闽菜 湘菜 徽菜 鲁

湘菜 徽菜 苏菜

菜 鲁菜 粤菜 川

徽菜 鲁菜 粤菜

菜 闽菜 湘菜 徽

湘菜 徽菜 浙菜

菜 粤菜 川菜 苏

菜 徽菜 鲁菜 粤

包子家族
BAO FAMILY

RECIPES FROM THE EIGHT CULINARY REGIONS OF CHINA

CÉLINE CHUNG

Photographs by Grégoire Kalt
Styling by Agathe Hernandez
Artistic direction by Atelier Choque Le Goff
Preface by Catherine Roig

murdoch books
London | Sydney

I DEDICATE THIS BOOK
IN PARTICULAR TO BILLY PHAM,
WHO IS BY MY SIDE IN MAKING
MY DREAMS A REALITY,
AND TO ALL OUR CHEFS
WHO HAVE SHARED THEIR
FAVOURITE RECIPES.

A SPECIAL MENTION
TO THE CHUNG FAMILY,
MY FATHER RUI YAO CHUNG,
MY MOTHER XIANXUE CHUNG,
AND MY BROTHER CHRISTIAN
CHUNG, WHO TAUGHT ME
TO ENJOY THE DISHES OF
OUR CUISINE, SHARE OUR
TABLES AND LOOK AFTER
THE STOMACHS
AND HEALTH OF THOSE
WHO ARE DEAR TO US.
THEY HAVE TAUGHT
ME THAT THE REAL WAY
TO THE HEART IS THROUGH
THE STOMACH.

包子家族

Just the right combination of talent and energy was needed to reinvent Chinese restaurants in Paris. It also took boldness to face the most appalling stereotypes head on, proclaiming at the Gros Bao opening: '*No cats, no rats, just Chinese food!*' Céline Chung brings all this to the table as well as one more special ingredient: her bicultural identity. Born in Paris, but originally from Wenzhou (south of Shanghai) she is the epitome of today's global citizen. The kind of young woman that success stories are made of on the big screen. Brilliant, determined, creative, multilingual and community minded, Céline turns everything she touches to gold … and she is just getting started! So far she has created casual dining at Petit Bao, bringing a Parisian touch to Shanghai xiao long bao (or XLB), while Gros Bao's red-accented décor is perfect for enjoying the most delectable of Chinese specialities, such as Sichuan mapo tofu, sheng jian bao or Peking duck. Céline discovered these delicacies when she travelled through China as a business school student, taking her back to her roots and with a single goal: to eat! As with any self-respecting Chinese family, for the Chungs, food is a religion, where love is demonstrated not through words but through cooking. Daily. Generously. Sublimely.

Céline returned with her head bursting with feelings, memories and inspiration, her entrepreneurial spirit calling her to create the kind of Chinese restaurant that didn't yet exist in Paris. A restaurant that was neither an overpriced palace nor a hole-in-the-wall that can't tell the difference between a spring roll and a dim sum. Just a relaxed, delicious, modern place for everyone. If Gros Bao's phenomenal popularity is anything to go by, this vision has clearly been a success: you'll need to come armed with patience to get a table. Like many, I waited patiently. And in the weeks that followed, I couldn't stop thinking about the melt-in-your-mouth eggplants and their secret sauce, the spring onion pancakes, the charsiu bao and many other dishes that made me want to meet Céline and her team: Lucy, Diana, Jessica, Carole, Billy and the others. Meeting them is like biting into a sweet chilli – it's an explosion of spice and heat, but in a graceful and subtle way. Just like their cooking that you will discover in this book, they are full of joy and happiness. The cherry on top of the bao: many recipes are easy, dispelling preconceived ideas about Chinese cuisine, or rather Chinese cuisines. *Xie xie* and long live the Bao Family!

Catherine Roig

包子家族

引言

INTRO-
DUCTION
9

包子家族

包子家族

BAO FAMILY

包子家族

COOKING, OUR LOVE LANGUAGE, BY CÉLINE CHUNG

FRANCO-CHINESE CULTURE

China and France are intertwined parts of my story. I was actually born in Paris, but both my parents are from China. My father arrived in France when he was sixteen and my mother joined him at the age of nineteen, just after their marriage. At home, my mother spoke the dialect of Wenzhou, our home town (a city in Zhejiang province, south of Shanghai), while my father spoke French to us.

It was my grandfather who first settled in France. After a series of odd jobs, he managed to save enough money for his family to make a decent living. He opened ETS Chung, a leather goods store located in the Marais district on rue Saint-Merri, in the heart of Paris.

We lived in Paris, in the 3rd district, and then at my grandfather's house in Bry-sur-Marne (to the east of Paris). My mother, who had learned to cook alongside my grandmother, prepared traditional meals for lunch and dinner. It was a mild and slightly sweet cuisine, which uses soy sauce and Shaoxing wine as a base and is mainly comprised of vegetables and steamed fish. My mother's favourite dish was steamed sea bass with soy sauce, sprinkled with ginger and spring onion.

Up until the age of ten, I had only tasted my mother's cooking. It was at this age that I discovered the canteen at primary school, which opened up another world to me. One of bread, chips, macaroni and yoghurt! And when I invited my friends home, it was their turn to discover a whole new world. They learned to eat with chopsticks and were amazed by all the flavours they tasted for the first time.

At that point, what I knew about Chinese culture (and cooking) was what I had learned from my family members.

A FRESH LOOK AT CHINESE CULTURE AND CUISINE

At the age of twenty, I had an irrepressible desire to discover China with my own eyes; to get away from the vision my parents had passed on to me and to form my own view of this country and this culture that I actually knew little about. As part of my business school studies, I chose to do a university exchange in Shanghai. It was the ideal opportunity to perfect my Mandarin, live like a local, discover the country and, importantly, the diversity of its cuisine!

I was swept up in curiosity and excitement as soon as I moved to Shanghai. I wandered through the streets, all my senses on the lookout ... I meandered through the city, intoxicated by the smells of food that filled the alleys from morning to evening, between the hole-in-the-wall restaurants and the fruit and vegetable stalls in the middle of the street, surrounded by Chinese people walking around holding something to eat, even striding through the corridors of the subway with their bags of take-away food. Food was everywhere! I set out to taste everything from breakfast to dinner, testing out all kinds of restaurants in Shanghai. It was a real culinary awakening! I also had the opportunity to travel to other parts of China: Yunnan, Sichuan, Beijing, Guangzhou and Hong Kong. Each has its own cultural and culinary identity. Flavours, products and cooking methods differ in each region. This means that you can't talk about Chinese cuisine, but rather Chinese cuisines.

包子家族

包子家族

CHINESE CUISINE:
A WAY OF LIFE

Chinese cuisines are complex, flavourful, full of textures, sweet, salty, sour and spicy; so delicious, yet so little known. Certain produce is favoured depending on the season, and Chinese medicine traditions are respected. Food holds a key place because it defines the rhythm of the day.

As a child, I had the opportunity to visit my grandparents in China, in their native village of Wenzhou. The days consisted mainly of going to eat noodles in the morning at the hole-in-the-wall on the shopping street, €2 for a comforting bowl of hot noodles; then we would head to the market to buy vegetables and meat to prepare lunch and dinner. Afterwards, it took over an hour to cook all the dishes to be shared for lunch and then we feasted on them for at least two hours. There was Peking duck, stir-fried vegetables, noodles, steamed fish and fruit on the table. In the afternoon, we played and ran around the courtyard of the house or had a nap, waiting for evening and dinnertime. Ultimately, the day revolved around the meals and nothing else. As a child, I didn't understand this rhythm. I found that every day was the same, it bored me and I had the impression that life was all about eating. Growing up, I realised that meals are everything in a Chinese family, the ultimate proof of love. Meals represent a time when we care for others, show them our love – a time for sharing, exchanging ideas, having great conversations and making decisions. Cooking in China means more than just eating, it's a way of life!

BAO FAMILY: A BRIDGE BETWEEN TWO CULTURES, BETWEEN TRADITION AND MODERNITY

When I finished my studies, I started a run-of-the-mill consulting career. I soon got bored and realised that what I was doing had no meaning for me. I had always wanted to do something entrepreneurial that was close to my heart. When I started thinking about it, the Chinese restaurant idea took hold of me and I immediately knew it was what I had to do. When I returned from Shanghai, my only desire was to rediscover the cuisine I had tasted there, in a place where I could spend special moments with my loved ones. But I couldn't find this place, and that's how the idea to create the restaurant of my dreams was born! It would serve authentic traditional Chinese cuisine with classic dishes, from French-sourced products as much as possible, in a modern setting with design inspired by Paris and Shanghai. I wanted to reproduce the art and way of eating in China: tables filled with communal plates, where everyone tastes and shares each dish.

Bao would be the star product, because it's timeless and requires great skill to make. It's also perfect to eat at any time during the day, whether you're hungry or not! Most importantly, I wanted to break with the unfashionable clichéd image of this cuisine and make it trendy and for everyone.

We opened Petit Bao in January 2019, on rue Saint-Denis in the 2nd district, just a stone's throw from the area where I grew up. We took over a Chinese deli, and it was like returning to my childhood and adding our own our modern touch. It was all about respecting traditions and bringing them up to date. Respecting the kitsch codes that we love, and giving them a contemporary feel.

Gros Bao, our second restaurant, located on the Canal Saint-Martin in the 10th district, embodies this concept completely. It is this fusion of tradition and modernity that drives us daily, in our cooking, our spaces and our visual identity.

包子家族

FROM RESTAURANT TO COOKBOOK

I wanted to open restaurants because I wanted to bring happiness to as many people as possible. Our days can sometimes be difficult, but when you eat something good, it puts a smile on your face and brings us back to what matters most: enjoying yourself, sharing time with your loved ones, awakening your senses and travelling. Chinese cuisine is a sharing cuisine, so Bao Family is a sharing project. We share everything we love to make you happy and transport you to China in our restaurants. And now you can travel in your own home too! These recipes have been created and adapted by our chefs so that you can explore China, from breakfast to dinner.
The real way to the heart is through the stomach!

包子家族

LUCY CHEN

Chinese cuisine is generous but doesn't waste anything. It shows a fierce willingness to respect traditional techniques but often in unorthodox ways. It's a cuisine where years of preparation are necessary to master a technique that takes just a minute to execute. It's hearing at the same time: 'You should really pay attention to your weight,' and, 'Have a little more, please.' But above all, Chinese cuisine is undivided dedication!

It was only after cooking with chefs from around the world that I realised that these apparent contradictions are in fact characteristics of Chinese chefs, characteristics that also come through in their cooking. When I'm in a Chinese kitchen, I can clearly hear the sound of garlic and ginger cooking in a perfectly seasoned wok. I can feel steam escaping from the bamboo baskets on my face. And when I finally sit down at the table to eat, I can taste the special flavours that are the soul of this cuisine that I love so much, a soul I'm convinced will survive the test of time and changes in recipes or techniques.

LESLIE CHIRINO

Chinese cuisine is about respect. Respect for a culture so rich and different from mine, for its ingredients and for the people I work alongside daily in the restaurant. It's also about challenges, discovering new flavours and combinations every day and trying new techniques. But above all, it's about always seeking to learn and grow. For me, this is a pivotal part of my passion for food and cooking.

包子家族

JESSICA CHAN

I see Chinese food first and foremost as comfort and nostalgia. My grandparents are Hakka people from the Guangdong province who migrated to Hong Kong in the 1950s. Growing up, Cantonese and Hakka food was a big part of my life. My grandparents loved to cook. Food brought everyone around the table to share stories from their day at work and school. Chinese food to me means family, community and gathering.

Chinese food now also represents adventure and discovery for the senses: sights, smells, tastes and even sounds make up these exciting culinary experiences. I love the diversity and long history behind the cuisine. China covers a vast geographical area, and each region has its own identity with unique flavour profiles, characterised by the meats, vegetables, condiments and sauces that are special to the terroir of each place.

Lastly, Chinese food is resourceful and humble. I admire that recipes are created to respect produce and ingredients by using every part of them. The cuisine reflects the creativity and spirit of its people.

包子家族

LIMING SHU

《中餐》是中华民族的具有独特风味的饮食文化；是渊源流长的中华五千多年的文明历史的宝贵遗产！如今, 它融合了古今中外的烹饪精华, 深受国内外朋友的追捧和青睐！成为世界饮食文化宝库中的一颗璀璨的明珠！
其色、香、味均应具全的饮食荟萃而风靡全球！
君若未尝, 乃生平一憾！

'Chinese cuisine' is an essential and unique part of Chinese culture. It's a precious heritage made up of five thousand years of civilisation and history!

Nowadays, Chinese cuisine combines the essence of traditional cuisine with foreign cuisines, ancient customs and modern practices. It's highly sought after and appreciated by friends, both here and abroad. It's becoming a shining pearl among the treasures of international culinary culture!

With its colours, scents and tastes offering a wide range of dishes, it's popular all over the world.

If you haven't tasted it yet, you might regret it all your life!

VICTOR ZHENG

With the agricultural revolution, people became more sedentary and started relying on each other to source food. Since then they have, however, never stopped migrating, travelling away from their childhood homes and moving to other countries. When they move away, they seek to preserve the legacy of their ancestors. They try to reproduce what is familiar to them and take new ingredients with them. All this leads to boundless creativity and culinary diversity.

Every time I ask myself where I come from, I also set out to find the origin of the flavours. The smell coming from the kitchen, the ingredients lined up on the bench or the utensils hanging on the wall. Cooking taught me Chinese ethics, the philosophy of well-being and the aesthetics of cooking. I grow up, I love, I leave and I find myself.

In the end, I chose to be a chef to make the connection between the home and cooking. For me, eating together as a family is the simplest desire of all Chinese people. And no matter where I am, I can always recall the flavours of home, of my apartment in China.

包子家族

包子家族

TENZIN

Chinese food to me is one of the healthiest around. It must be fresh, with lots of vegetables. Many of the ingredients serve medicinal purposes. Chinese meals are shared communally, with dishes placed in the centre of the table, friends and family seated around with their rice bowls. You'll rarely see a knife and fork at a Chinese table as they use chopsticks instead. How do they cut meat? No need to, ingredients are prepared bite-sized and ready-to-eat with chopsticks. In China, every province has its own culinary traditions. These traditions, combined with the number of cooking methods that exist (steaming, stewing, stir-frying, roasting), mean that ingredients in Chinese cuisine can be prepared in so many ways!

MADAME CHUN

What is Chinese cuisine? There are different Chinese cuisines. Each region has a different cuisine and different flavours.
Whether they are fried, stir-fried or simmered, all the dishes are delicious. Chinese dishes are extremely varied, they can be savoury or sweet, meat-based or vegetarian, showcasing treasures of the land as well as the sea. Their colours, aromas and tastes come together to provide a rich, rounded culinary experience. Simply put, Chinese cuisine has a long history, is multifaceted and delicious.

包子家族

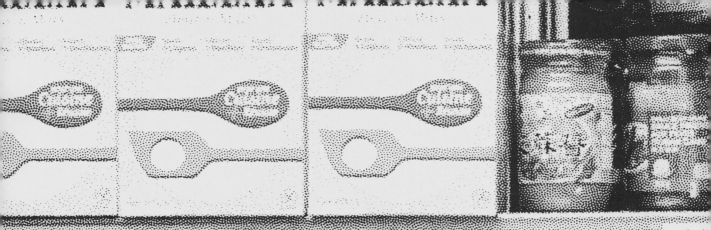

MIRIN

RICE VINEGAR

SESAME OIL

包子家族

酱料
CONDIMENTS, THICK SAUCES & PASTES

LAO GAN MA / LǍO GĀN MĀ .... 老干妈

A brand of chilli oil well known in China and around the world. We use *crispy chilli oil* that contains chillies, fermented soybeans, garlic and onions. It can be used in recipes or as a condiment to accompany dishes.

FERMENTED GARLIC AND BEAN SAUCE / SUÀN RÓNG DÒUCHǏ JIÀNG .... 蒜蓉豆豉酱

A sauce made with black fermented soybeans and garlic, it can be used in stir-fried dishes or steamed dishes. It works well with seafood.

SPICY FERMENTED BEAN PASTE/ LÀ DÒU BÀN JIÀNG .... 辣豆瓣酱

Doubanjiang is a chilli paste made from fermented bean sprouts and soybeans. It is chunky, red and brown in colour and contains umami, salty and spicy flavours. It is widely used in the cuisine of the Sichuan region. For example, oil is heated in the wok, then doubanjiang is added and fried as a base for mapo tofu sauce.

SWEET FERMENTED BEAN SAUCE / TIÁN MIÀN JIÀNG ....甜面酱

Tianmianjiang is a dark, thick sauce that mainly contains fermented wheat flour and sometimes soybeans, contrary to what its name might suggest. It is often used for making zhajiang mian, and adds a sweet, salty and umami taste.

SESAME PASTE / ZHĪ MA JIÀNG ....芝麻酱

Unlike tahini, which uses raw white sesame seeds, this sesame paste is made with toasted sesame seeds. It is therefore darker and has a richer flavour. It is used in sauces for cold noodles or as a base for sauces served with Chinese hot pot.

HOISIN SAUCE / HǍIXIĀN JITO NG ....海鲜酱

This thick and dark fermented soybean paste is commonly used in Cantonese cuisine, in marinades for rotisseries or simply as sauce served alongside Peking duck.

CONDENSED MILK / LIÀNRǓ .... 炼乳

Smooth and sweet, it is often used in drinks, such as Hong Kong milk tea, or in desserts.

FERMENTED BLACK BEANS / DÒUCHǏ .... 豆豉

Fermented, whole and dried black soybeans are used as a base for fermented soy sauce, but they can also be used whole in sautéed or braised dishes.

FERMENTED YELLOW SOYBEAN PASTE / HUÁNGDÒU JIÀNG ....黄豆浆

A sauce made from fermented yellow soybeans. It is widely used in the Beijing area and in northern Chinese cuisine. It is used in particular in the preparation of zhajiang mian.

包子家族

酱汁
LIQUID CONDIMENTS

SESAME OIL / ZHĪ MA YÓU .... 芝麻油

Sesame oil can be made from toasted or untoasted sesame seeds. Toasted seeds add a lot of flavour to dishes, which is why we prefer to use this oil. It can be used in marinades or added at the end of cooking, as it should not be heated too much.

RICE VINEGAR / MI CÙ .... 米醋

A transparent vinegar made from fermented rice that is quite mild and not as strong as a white vinegar. It can be used to add acidity to stir-fried dishes or sauces.

YONGCHUN VINEGAR / YǑNGCHŪN LǍO CU .... 永春老醋

Black vinegar made from fermented glutinous rice, used for marinating cold dishes, preparing braised dishes or simply as a dipping sauce for dumplings. Chinkiang is another popular black vinegar.

OYSTER SAUCE / HÁO YÓU .... 蚝油

A dark-coloured sauce with a thick texture. Oyster sauce is mainly used in Cantonese cuisine and adds flavour and umami to dishes. It is used in marinades and sauces or in stir-fried dishes.

LIGHT SOY SAUCE / SHĒNG CHŌU .... 生抽

Light soy sauce is a key ingredient in Chinese cuisine. It has a light colour and liquid texture and is used to salt and season dishes.

DARK SOY SAUCE / LǍO CHŌU .... 老抽

Dark soy sauce is darker and has a more syrupy texture and is also slightly sweeter than light soy sauce. As it is less salty, it is mainly used to add colour to dishes.

SHAOXING WINE/ SHÀO XĪNG HUĀ DIĀO JIU .... 紹興花雕酒

Chinese rice wine is originally from Shaoxing city in the Zhejiang province. It is made by fermenting rice with water and a little wheat. There are several types – some are consumed directly as alcohols (those that are fermented longer) and others of lesser quality and with added salt are used for cooking. This wine adds depth and complexity to dishes. It is used in marinades or in fillings (wontons and dumplings), during wok cooking, to deglaze and flavour sautéed dishes or to add taste to simmered dishes.

包子家族

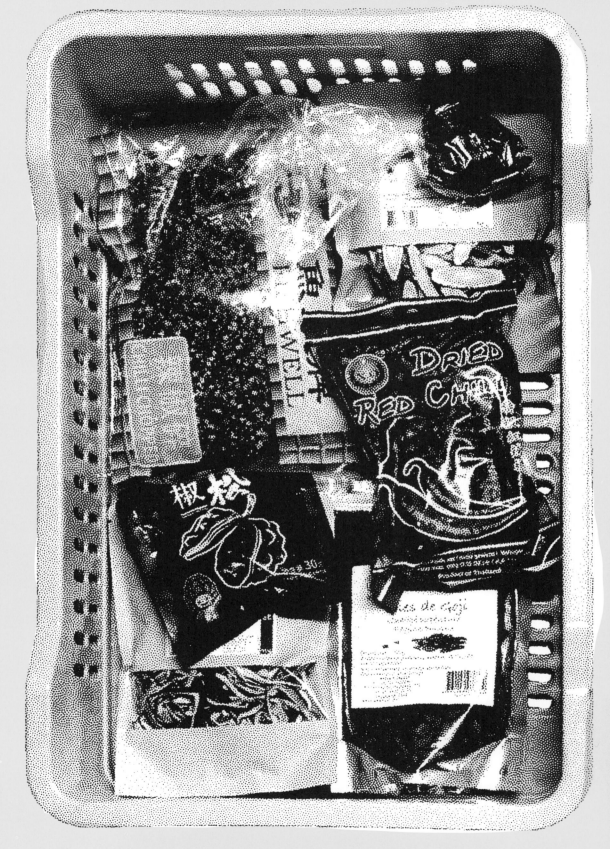

包子家族

包子家族

香料
SPICES

DRIED CHILLIES / GĀN LÀJIĀO .... 干辣椒

Dried whole chillies are widely used in Sichuan cuisine.

CHILLI POWDER / LÀJIĀO MIÀN ....辣椒麵

A powder made from roasted and dried chillies. It is used to add spice to dishes.

SICHUAN PEPPER / HUĀJIĀO .... 花椒

With a fresh aroma and citrus notes, Sichuan pepper comes in green or red pepper varieties and can be used whole, toasted or ground. Sichuan powder is used in marinades or in cooking and to add flavour to sautéed dishes. It is also what gives you a tingly, numbing sensation.

ORANGE PEEL / CHÉNPÍ .... 陳皮

Orange peel is used together with other spices to make broths, stews and various simmered dishes.

LIQUORICE / GĀNCĂO .... 甘草

Often found in thinly sliced form, it is used in spice mixtures such as when making soups.

STAR ANISE / BĀJIĂO .... 八角

Star-shaped and slightly red-brown in colour, it adds an aniseed taste to dishes. Be mindful to use it sparingly.

GOJI BERRIES / GŎUQĬZĬ .... 枸杞子

Goji berries have many benefits, which means they are often used in soups or hearty dishes.

包子家族

包子家族

经典食材
STAPLE INGREDIENTS

CENTURY EGGS / PÍ DÀN .... 皮蛋

Century eggs are mostly made with duck eggs that are kept for a few weeks, or even a few months, in a mixture that includes lime, paddy rice (unhusked rice), ash, salt and tea leaves. The egg white takes on a translucent brown colour and a jelly-like texture and the yolk becomes creamy and dark green.

SALTED EGGS / XIÁNDÀN .... 咸蛋

Salted eggs can be raw or cooked and are made using duck eggs soaked in brine.

SILKEN TOFU / NÈNDÒUFU .... 嫩豆腐

Made from soybeans, silken tofu is neither drained nor pressed and still contains a lot of water.

FIRM TOFU / LĀODÒUFU .... 老豆腐

Firm tofu is drained and pressed, but still contains some water.

WOOD EAR MUSHROOMS / MÙ'ĚR .... 木耳

Mushrooms with a crunchy texture and a subtle taste, which easily take on other flavours.

SHIITAKE MUSHROOMS / XIĀNG GŪ .... 香菇

Mostly found in dried form in Asian grocery stores. When they are rehydrated, strong umami flavours emerge. The soaking water is kept to prepare soups and other stews.

PICKLED MUSTARD GREENS / SUĀNCÀI .... 酸菜

Pickled mustard greens are often used in soups or stir-fried dishes. They add a lot of flavour and depth to dishes.

HULLED MUNG BEANS / LÚ DÒU .... 绿豆

Mung beans can be eaten in seed or sprouted form. When they are used as seeds, they are for making soups or creams (sweet fillings). Once they are sprouted, they are known as bean sprouts, which are eaten in salads or stir-fried.

BLACK SESAME SEEDS / HĒI ZHĪMA .... 黑芝麻

Sesame seeds are mostly toasted. They can be used as a garnish or for making dishes and desserts.

包子家族

包子家族

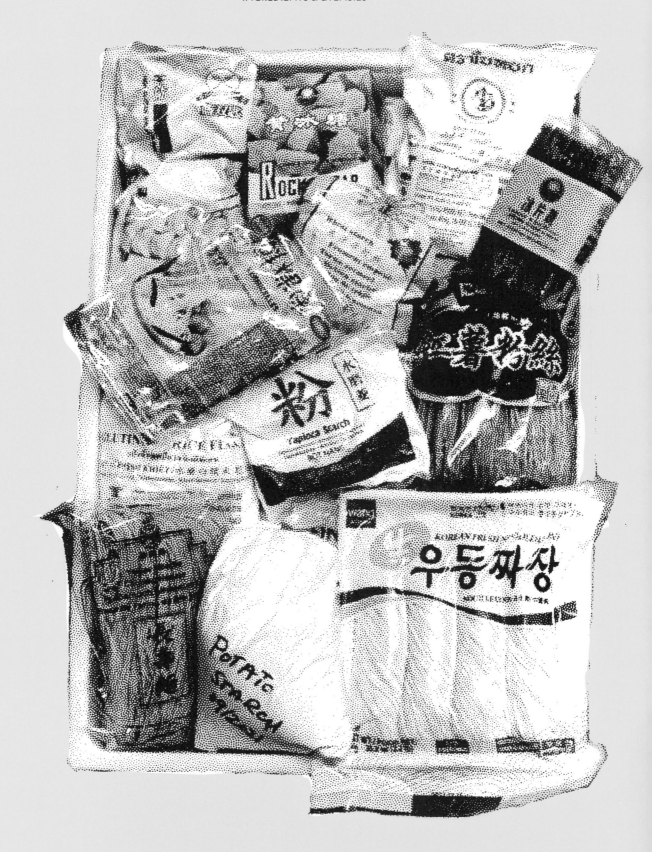

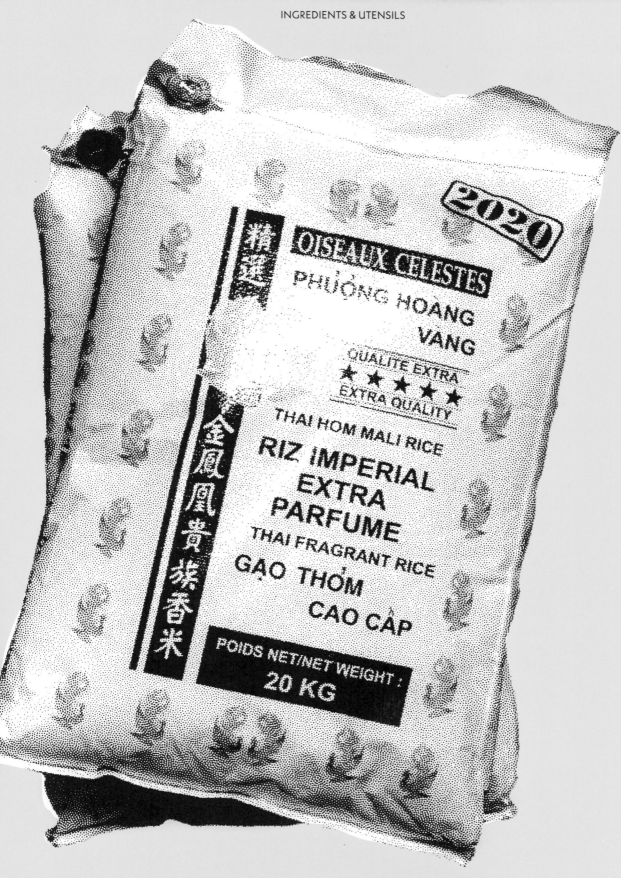

包子家族

淀粉 面粉 糖
STARCHES, FLOURS & SUGARS

WHEAT STARCH / XIǍOMÀI DIÀNFĚN ....小麦淀粉

When mixed with a liquid and heated, wheat starch becomes translucent and slightly sticky. It is mainly used in combination with rice flour and other starches to make dim sum, such as har gow or cheungfun.

POTATO STARCH / TǓDÒU DIÀNFĚN ....土豆淀粉

Used as a thickener, to prepare breading or to make noodles, for example.

RICE FLOUR / NIÁN MǏ FĚN ....粘米粉

Made from very finely ground rice, it is used to make rice cakes or radish cakes (luo bo gao).

GLUTINOUS (STICKY) RICE FLOUR / NUÒ MǏ FĚN ....糯米粉

Similar in appearance to rice flour, glutinous rice flour gives a sticky texture. It is used in many dim sum and dessert recipes.

TAPIOCA FLOUR / MÙ SHǓ FĚN ....木薯粉

Tapioca flour (starch) is extracted from cassava roots and can be used to thicken sauces, make rice noodles or dumpling dough or to get the sticky and elastic texture found in desserts such as taro balls.

CANE SUGAR / ZHÈ TÁNG ....蔗糖

Cane sugar adds a more complex and vanilla taste than white sugar.

ROCK SUGAR / BĪNG TANG ....冰糖

Sold in the form of irregular pieces that can be white or transparent yellow and are less sweet than normal caster sugar. Rock sugar can be used in savoury dishes to counterbalance salt and bring flavours together or to create a glossy finish. It is also used for making desserts.

包子家族

包子家族

面和米
NOODLES & RICE

RICE NOODLES / HÉFĚN .... 河粉
Wide noodles made from rice flour and tapioca or corn starch.

FINE YELLOW NOODLES/ CHÁNGSHÒU ....长寿面
Thin wheat noodles with a yellow colour that comes from turmeric.

RAMEN NOODLES / LĀMIÀN .... 拉面
Wheat noodles.

JASMINE RICE / XIĀNGMĬ .... 香米
Soft, thick and fragrant rice grains to be cooked in a rice cooker. Wash the rice three times before cooking. For the right amount of water and optimal results, when you immerse your fist into the rice covered with water, the water should reach your fingertips.

SWEET POTATO VERMICELLI / HÓNGSHŬ FĚNSĪ .... 红薯粉丝
Long, dark-grey vermicelli noodles, which become translucent and light after cooking.

包子家族

包子家族

包子家族

包子家族

包子家族

BAO FAMILY

包子家族

新鲜食材
FRESH PRODUCE

LEBANESE EGGPLANT (AUBERGINE) / QIÉ ZI .... 茄子

Eggplants that are longer and thinner than those usually found in the West. They should be firm and dense when purchased.

SPRING ONION / XIĀNG CŌNG .... 香葱

Spring onion stems (or scallions) are commonly used in Chinese cuisine. They can be the feature ingredient in dishes, such as spring onion pancakes or Shanghai noodles, or they can be used in marinades or as a garnish.

CORIANDER / XIĀNG CÀI .... 香菜

Coriander is widely used in Chinese cuisine. It adds taste and a hint of freshness to dishes. Leaves and stems are used.

BEAN SPROUTS / DÒU YÁ .... 豆芽

These are often stir-fried in wok dishes together with other ingredients.

WATER SPINACH / KŌNG XĪN CÀI .... 空心菜

Long hollow stems, with small, thin dark-green leaves at the end.

CHINESE BROCCOLI OR GAI LAN / JIÈ LÁN .... 芥兰

Recognisable by its long light green stems and wide dark green leaves.

GARLIC CHIVES / JIŬ CÀI .... 韭菜

Dark-green long and flat leaves with a very pronounced taste and strong smell. They are primarily eaten cooked.

YARDLONG BEANS / JIĀNG DÒU .... 豇豆

Denser and crunchier than green beans, they are mostly stir-fried in a wok.

GARLIC SCAPES / SUÀNMIÁO .... 蒜苗

These long green shoots are often used as side.

WINTER MELON OR WAX GOURD / DŌNG GUĀ .... 冬瓜

Contrary to what its name suggests, winter melon is actually a variety of squash. It has white flesh, a very mild taste and is mostly used in soups.

LOTUS ROOT / LIÁN ŎU .... 莲藕

Choose firm and fresh roots and wash them thoroughly before cooking.

CHINESE CABBAGE OR PE-TSAÏ / DÀ BÁI CÀI .... 大白菜

Chinese cabbage has long light-green leaves. Soft and easy to cook, it is often used in soups, stir-fries or dumplings.

SHIITAKE MUSHROOMS / XIĀNG GŪ .... 香菇

Fresh mushrooms with a buttery flavour.

ENOKI MUSHROOMS / JĪN ZHĒN GŪ ......金针菇

Small, long and thin white mushrooms, with a crunchy texture. They are often used in stir-fried dishes or in soups.

DAIKON / LUÓ BO .... 萝卜

Long white radish that is eaten raw or cooked. Choose heavy ones with nice green leaves. Known in Southern Asia as mooli.

包子家族

包子家族

中式厨房用具
BASIC UTENSILS

STEAMER BASKET / SHĀOJĪ .... 筲箕

Mainly used to steam-cook food, it can also serve as a colander, container or even as a serving dish.

CLEAVER / CÀIDĀO .... 菜刀

An essential knife in any Chinese cuisine that can be used for almost anything. It can be made of carbon steel or stainless steel.

LADLE / GUŌ CHǍN .... 锅铲

A ladle is very useful for wok cooking. It is used to stir, pour liquids into the wok during cooking or transfer cooked ingredients onto plates.

ROLLING PIN / GĂN MIÀN ZHÀNG .... 擀麵杖

A wooden rolling pin that is thinner than a traditional pastry rolling pin. Its shape makes it easier to hold when rolling out rounds of bao dough.

ROUND SLOTTED SKIMMER SPOON / SPIDER / LOÙ PIÁO .... 漏瓢

This type of spoon makes it easy to remove noodles or dumplings after cooking in water or oil.

CHOPSTICKS / KUÀI ZI .... 筷子

Chopsticks are often used to mix ingredients or to separate them when frying.

METAL SPATULA / DĂ XIÀN CHǏ .... 打馅尺

A spatula mainly used to spread dumpling or xiao long bao filling onto the dough. It is optional and you can easily use a spoon instead.

WOK / CHĂO GUŌ .... 炒鍋

A wok is another essential utensil. It is used for all stir-fried dishes, but also for frying, steaming or boiling. Its curved base allows both the heat and ingredients to be evenly distributed. For the most part, it is made of cast iron or carbon steel. It can have a long handle, two side handles, or a long handle and a side handle, depending on its main use.

There are a number of tutorials and information online to learn how to season a wok before its first use, as well as what kind of tools should be used to clean it. For home use, the best method is to take the rough side of a sponge and gently rub the wok under water with a little soap, until there is no more food on the surface of the wok. If food remains stuck or the wok is particularly greasy, you can pour hot water into it to soften the remaining food or to degrease the surface. Next, rinse it under water and dry it inside and out with a tea towel. Put the wok back on the heat to remove any remaining moisture, then turn off the heat. Use paper towel with a little vegetable oil on it to coat the whole wok in a thin layer of oil. What to remember: ❶ Do not rub the wok too hard, just enough for the surface to be clean. ❷ It is not necessary to leave the wok over very high heat, and oil over the whole surface, as may be the case in a professional kitchen. ❸ Make sure that the wok is always perfectly dry, otherwise it may rust and you will have to treat it before using it next.

包子家族

包子家族

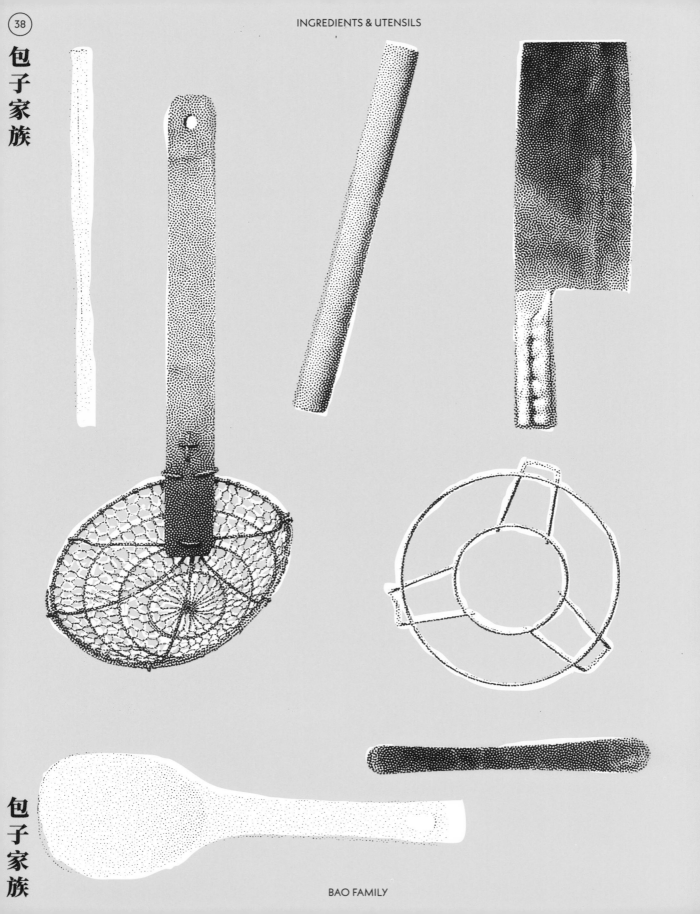

包子家族

包子家族

包子家族

早饭

BREAKFAST
41

皮蛋瘦肉粥
CONGEE WITH CENTURY EGG

MAKES AROUND 5 SERVINGS

INGREDIENTS

RICE ....400 G (2 CUPS)
WATER ....2.5 LITRES (10 CUPS)
PORK NECK...100 G (3½ OZ)
CENTURY EGGS ....3 OR 4
SALT...TO YOUR TASTE
WHITE PEPPER ....4 PINCHES
LIGHT SOY SAUCE.......................................A FEW DROPS
SESAME OIL...A FEW DROPS

GARNISH
CHOPPED CORIANDER OR SPRING ONION

❶ Pour the rice into a large saucepan and rinse it. ● Pour in the water and bring to a boil, then cook, covered, over low heat for 30 minutes.

❷ Meanwhile, thinly slice the pork and cut the century eggs into quarters and then into small pieces.

❸ Take the lid off the congee and add the pork and eggs. ● Leave to simmer for 2 to 3 minutes over medium to high heat. ● Add salt, white pepper and soy sauce, to your taste. ● Add a few drops of sesame oil, garnish with fresh herbs or spring onion and serve.

油条
YOUTIAO

MAKES AROUND 12 PIECES

INGREDIENTS

PLAIN FLOUR	500 G (3⅓ CUPS)
BAKING POWDER	12 G (½ OZ)
SALT	6 G (⅛ OZ)
BICARBONATE OF SODA	3 G (⅛ OZ)

EGG	1
ICED WATER	280–290 ML (10 FL OZ)
VEGETABLE OIL	2 TABLESPOONS + FOR FRYING

❶ Mix the flour, baking powder, salt and bicarbonate of soda in a large bowl. ● Whisk the egg, water and 2 tablespoons of oil together in a bowl and gently mix the liquid into the dry ingredients. ● Mix until a smooth dough is obtained, cover with plastic wrap and leave in a damp place for 1 hour 30 minutes.

❷ Work the dough a second time by kneading it, then let it rest for another 45 minutes.

❸ Heat the frying oil to 180°C (350°F). ● Meanwhile, roll out the dough on an oiled benchtop to form a 1 cm (½ inch) thick rectangle, then cut it into 3 × 9 cm (1¼ × 3½ inch) strips. ● Stack two strips on top of each other and press down firmly all the way down the length using a Chinese chopstick.

❹ Holding both ends, carefully drop each youtiao into the oil. ● Turn constantly for 30 seconds so that it cooks evenly on all sides, then remove from the oil. ● Be sure to remove excess oil by draining the youtiao on paper towel.

❺ Lovely served with hot or cold soy milk.

包
子
家
族

早饭

煎蛋饭
FRIED EGG ON RICE

WE LIKE TO USE FRIED SHALLOTS, DRIED PORK, SPRING ONION AND SESAME SEEDS AS A GARNISH.

MAKES 1 SERVING

INGREDIENTS	
RICE	1 BOWL
VEGETABLE OIL	1 TABLESPOON
EGG	1
SOY SAUCE	A DRIZZLE

GARNISH
CHOPPED CORIANDER OR SPRING ONION

❶ Cook a bowl of rice.

❷ Heat a frying pan over medium to high heat, then pour in the oil. ● Break the egg into the pan and cover. ● When the white begins to set, remove the lid and fry until the yolk reaches the desired consistency.

❸ Serve on top of the rice with a drizzle of soy sauce and add your choice of garnish.

包子家族

果酱炸馒头
MANTOU WITH JAM

SUPER SIMPLE BUT INCREDIBLY ADDICTIVE, THIS RECIPE IS IDEAL FOR USING LEFTOVER BAOZI DOUGH
(SEE PAGES 86–87) FROM THE PREVIOUS DAY AND STARTING THE DAY WITH A SWEET BREAKFAST.

INGREDIENTS
LEFTOVER BAOZI DOUGH
OIL FOR FRYING
JAM OR SUGAR

❶ Cut the dough into thick slices.

❷ Heat a frying pan over medium heat and pour in a drizzle of oil. ● Place the mantou slices in the pan and allow them to toast. ● Let them cook slowly (you can press lightly on the mantou so that the whole surface browns), until they are golden.

● Turn over and repeat on the other side (add a little more oil if necessary).

❸ Serve sprinkled with sugar or with your favourite jam.

包子家族

早饭

菠萝包
PINEAPPLE BUN

PINEAPPLE BUNS IN MANDARIN ARE CALLED 菠萝包 *BO LUO BAO* AND DO NOT CONTAIN PINEAPPLE, DESPITE THEIR NAME. THEY ARE SWEET BUNS WITH A CRACKER ON TOP THAT CAN BE USED AS A SANDWICH BUN, OR FILLED WITH A SWEET OR SAVOURY FILLING AND ACCOMPANIED BY A DRINK. THE APPEARANCE OF THE CRACKER, WHICH IS SOMETIMES RIDGED, IS REMINISCENT OF PINEAPPLE SKIN.

MAKES AROUND 10 BUNS

DOUGH	
BREAD FLOUR	200 G (1⅓ CUPS)
WHITE (GRANULATED) SUGAR	40 G (1½ OZ)
EGG	10 G (¼ OZ)
INSTANT DRIED YEAST	3 G (⅛ OZ)
MILK	100 ML (3½ FL OZ)
BUTTER (SEMI-SALTED)	20 G (¾ OZ)

TOPPING	
PLAIN FLOUR	100 G (⅔ CUP)
BAKING POWDER	¼ TEASPOON
BICARBONATE OF SODA	⅛ TEASPOON
MILK POWDER	5 G (⅛ OZ)
BUTTER	55 G (2 OZ)
WHITE (GRANULATED) SUGAR	45 G (1½ OZ)
BEATEN EGG	10 G (¼ OZ) + A LITTLE TO GLAZE

DOUGH PREPARATION

❶ Add all the dough ingredients except the butter to a stand mixer bowl, then knead using a dough hook until a smooth mixture is obtained. ● Add the diced butter and mix again until well combined. ● Cover and leave the dough to rest in a warm place until it doubles in volume.

❷ Place the dough on a lightly floured benchtop, then press gently to knock it down.

❸ Divide the dough into 10 portions of about 35 to 40 g (1¼ to 1½ oz), cover with a damp cloth or plastic wrap and allow to stand for 5 minutes.

❹ Form a ball with each piece of dough, place the balls on a baking tray, cover and leave to rise until they double in volume.

TOPPING PREPARATION

❶ Sift the flour, baking powder, bicarbonate of soda and milk powder into a bowl. ● Set aside.

❷ Cream the butter and sugar. ● Add the beaten egg and then the dry ingredients to form a smooth dough. ● Roll into a log and wrap in plastic wrap, then refrigerate for about 1 hour (or just enough time for it to firm up a little and become play-dough like in texture).

❸ Preheat the oven to 170°C (325°F). ● Divide the topping into 20 g (¾ oz) portions, place each portion between two sheets of baking paper and flatten with the palm of your hand (or a rolling pin).

❹ Brush each bun with beaten egg and gently place a portion of topping on top. ● Brush with egg again.

❺ Place on the bottom shelf of the oven and bake for 12 to 15 minutes, until the buns are golden brown.

包子家族

小吃

STARTERS
55

小吃

涼拌茄子
MARINATED SPICY EGGPLANT

FOR 2 TO 3 PEOPLE

INGREDIENTS
LEBANESE EGGPLANTS (AUBERGINES) ....600 G (1 LB 5OZ)
OIL FOR FRYING

MARINADE
MINCED GINGER ....100 G (3½ OZ)
MINCED GARLIC..100 G (3½ OZ)
WHITE (GRANULATED) SUGAR .... 80 G (2¾ OZ)
SESAME OIL ....3 TABLESPOONS
CORIANDER...1 STEM

CHOPPED SPRING ONION...............................2 TABLESPOONS
LEMON JUICE ....200 ML (7 FL OZ)
SOY SAUCE ....240 ML (8 FL OZ)
WATER..240 ML (8 FL OZ)
CHILLI OIL ....2 TABLESPOONS

GARNISH
SESAME SEEDS ....1 PINCH
FRESH RED CHILLI 1
CORIANDER (OPTIONAL)...........................1 SMALL HANDFUL

❶ Cut the eggplants into 10 × 2 cm (4 × ¾ inch) sticks. ● Fry them in oil at 160°C (320°F), until they are just cooked and their skin turns deep purple. ● Place them on paper towel to remove excess oil, then allow to cool. (If you prefer a lighter version, cook the eggplants in water, but their colour will not be as vibrant.)

❷ Combine the marinade ingredients and add the cooled eggplants. ● For the best result, leave the eggplants to marinate for at least 5 hours.

❸ Garnish with sesame seeds, finely chopped fresh chilli and coriander, if using.

包子家族

小吃

淹黄瓜
MARINATED CUCUMBERS

MAKES AROUND 10 SERVINGS

INGREDIENTS

CUCUMBER .... 500 G (1 LB 2 OZ)

MARINADE

GARLIC .... 60 G (2¼ OZ)
WHITE (GRANULATED) SUGAR .... 240 G (8½ OZ)
RICE VINEGAR .... 180 ML (¾ CUP)
SESAME OIL .... 90 ML (3 FL OZ)
SALT .... 45 G (1½ OZ)

GARNISH

SESAME SEEDS .... 1 PINCH
FRESH CHILLI 1
CHOPPED SPRING ONION .... 1 TEASPOON

❶ Finely chop the garlic. ● Combine all the marinade ingredients and set aside.

❷ Place the cucumber on a benchtop and crush it with the handle of a knife until it breaks in half. ● Separate the two pieces by hand and remove the seeds with a spoon. ● Use the same spoon to 'cut' the two halves into half-moon shapes, then place them all in a bowl.

❸ Pour the marinade over the cucumbers so that all the pieces are covered. ● Allow to stand for at least 1 hour 30 minutes, then enjoy. ● If you prefer a lightly seasoned cucumber, remove immediately, but you can leave the cucumber to marinate longer if you prefer more depth of flavour.

❹ Serve the cucumber pieces with a little marinade. ● Garnish with sesame seeds, chopped fresh chilli and spring onion.

OUR TIP
The marinade can be reused for other cucumbers! It can also be used as a salad dressing or in a cold noodle sauce.

包子家族

葱油煎饼
CHINESE SPRING ONION PANCAKES

MAKES AROUND 10 PANCAKES

PANCAKE DOUGH	
PLAIN FLOUR	500 G (3⅓ CUPS)
SALT	4 G (⅛ OZ)
INSTANT DRIED YEAST	2 G (¹⁄₁₆ OZ)
VEGETABLE OIL	2 TABLESPOONS
WATER AT 80°C (175°F)	250 ML (1 CUP)

FILLING	
SALT	½ TEASPOON
SESAME OIL	2 TABLESPOONS
PLAIN FLOUR	5 G (⅛ OZ)
SPRING ONION	3 STEMS

COOKING
OIL FOR FRYING

❶ Place the flour, salt, instant yeast, vegetable oil and water in a stand mixer bowl with a dough hook. ● Set the mixer at low speed for 8 minutes. ● Check that the dough is smooth and elastic. Continue mixing for another 1 to 2 minutes if necessary. ● Remove the dough from the mixer bowl and place it in a clean bowl. Cover loosely with plastic wrap or a slightly damp clean tea towel. ● Allow to stand at room temperature for 1 hour.

❷ Remove the dough from the bowl and knead it slowly. ● Divide the dough into two pieces, cover one half and set aside.

❸ Lightly flour your benchtop. ● Flatten the dough evenly into a wide 3–4 mm (⅛–³⁄₁₆ inch) thick oval shape. ● Make sure you roll out the dough gradually and patiently.

❹ Sprinkle 3 pinches of salt on the dough from a height, making sure it is evenly distributed. ● Run your fingers over the surface to 'feel' the seasoning of the dough. ● It should be light but evenly spread over the entire surface (you can always add more salt after cooking).

❺ Apply a thin layer of sesame oil to the entire surface of the dough with a pastry brush (or with your fingertips if you do not have one). ● Sprinkle 3 pinches of flour onto the dough. ● Spread the chopped spring onion evenly over the entire surface of the dough.

❻ Roll the dough from the bottom up into a tight log. ● Cut the dough into logs of around 80 g (2¾ oz) each. ● Pinch the ends of each small log, then twist each end in opposite directions (as if you were twisting a towel). ● Coil the twisted dough into a round spiral disc. ● Seal the outer end, then gently flatten the dough to ensure it keeps its shape. ● The thickness should be about 2 mm (¹⁄₁₆ inch) evenly across the whole circle. ● Allow to rest and repeat steps 3–6 with the remaining dough.

❼ Start with the first batch of coiled dough. ● Fry each pancake in a flat frying pan over medium heat, until the pancake bubbles are nicely golden and the surface is slightly golden. ● It is important that there is sufficient oil in the pan to cook both the surface and in between all the folds. ● Cut into quarters and serve.

小吃

蛋黄焗南瓜
PUMPKIN FRIES WITH SALTED EGG

MAKES AROUND 2 SERVINGS

INGREDIENTS

PUMPKIN .... 600 G (1 LB 5 OZ)
SALTED DUCK EGG YOLKS 2
CORNFLOUR .... 1 TABLESPOON
VEGETABLE OIL .... 1 TABLESPOON + FOR FRYING
SHAOXING WINE .... 1 TABLESPOON
CHOPPED SPRING ONION .... 1 SMALL HANDFUL
SALT

❶ Cut the pumpkin in half and remove all the seeds. ● Place the flat surface on a cutting board and carefully remove the skin. ● Cut the pumpkin into 1.5 cm (⅝ inch) thick slices, then slice to form fries. ● Salt the pumpkin slices (around 1 teaspoon) and allow to stand for at least 10 minutes so they release as much water as possible.

❷ Steam the egg yolks for 12 minutes, then crush them with a fork.

❸ Add the cornflour to the fries and mix so that each stick is coated. ● Fry them for 1 to 2 minutes in oil at 160°C (320°F) until the breading starts to become nice and golden. ● Remove from the oil and use paper towel to drain excess oil.

❹ Pour the vegetable oil into a frying pan over medium to high heat, then add the crushed egg yolks and stir. ● Pour in the Shaoxing wine and continue stirring until a foamy and smooth mixture is obtained. ● Add the pumpkin fries and stir to cover with the sauce. ● Add 1 pinch of salt, garnish with chopped spring onion and serve.

OUR TIP

Only the egg yolk is needed for this recipe. If you can't find already separated eggs, you can always buy whole eggs and separate the yolks from the whites.

包子家族

小吃

醉鸡
DRUNKEN CHICKEN WINGS

MAKES AROUND 2 SERVINGS

INGREDIENTS

WATER	2 LITRES (8 CUPS)
GINGER	5 SLICES
GARLIC	1 CLOVE
CHOPPED RED ASIAN SHALLOT	1
CHICKEN WINGS	10
SALT	1 TABLESPOON

SAUCE

BEER	200 ML (7 FL OZ)
BAY LEAF	1
SICHUAN RED PEPPERS	5
STAR ANISE	3
CINNAMON STICK	½
WHITE (GRANULATED) SUGAR	40 G (1½ OZ)
LIGHT SOY SAUCE	50 ML (1¾ FL OZ)
GOJI BERRIES	8
SHAOXING WINE	300 ML (10½ FL OZ)

❶ Heat all the sauce ingredients except the Shaoxing wine in a saucepan, then leave to cool. ● Once the liquid has cooled, pour in the wine.

❷ In a large saucepan of water, boil the ginger, garlic and chopped shallot. Add the chicken wings and salt and wait for the water to start boiling again. ● Leave to simmer for 6 minutes, then turn off the heat and leave to cook, covered, for another 6 minutes. ● Remove the chicken wings and immerse them in iced water (this will allow the skin to become firm).

❸ Place the chicken wings in the sauce and leave to marinate overnight. ● Serve cold.

包子家族

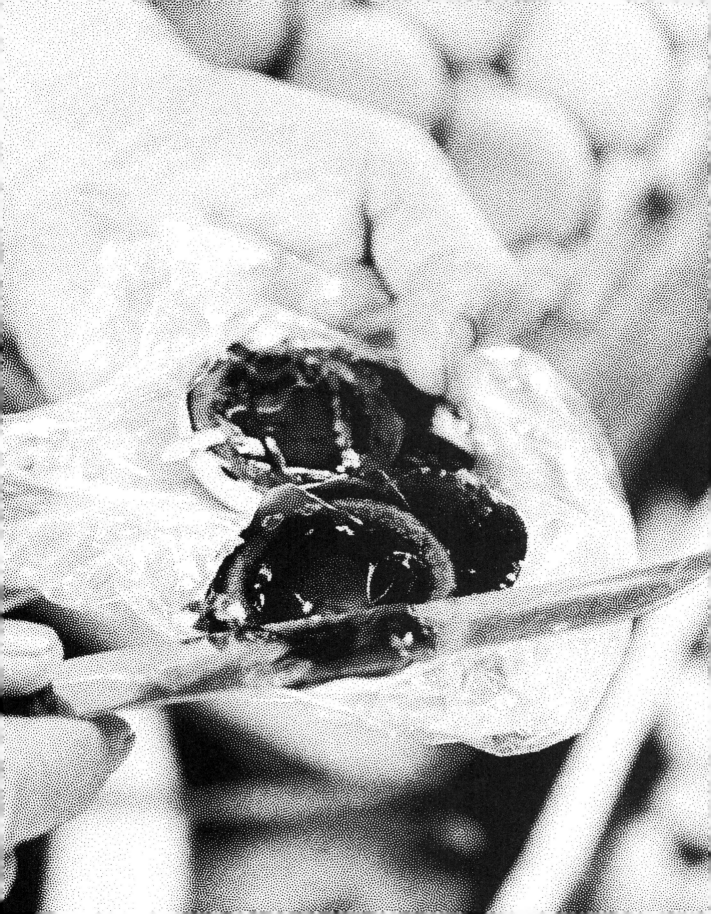

蚵仔煎
OYSTER OMELETTE

MAKES AROUND 2 SERVINGS

INGREDIENTS

EGGS	2
FISH SAUCE	1 TEASPOON + A LITTLE TO SERVE
WHITE PEPPER	A FEW PINCHES
TAPIOCA FLOUR (STARCH)	5 G (⅛ OZ)
CORNFLOUR	5 G (⅛ OZ)
WATER	80 ML (⅓ CUP)
VEGETABLE OIL	1 TABLESPOON
FRESH OYSTERS, SHUCKED	8 TO 10
CORIANDER	A FEW STEMS

❶ Break the eggs into a bowl, add 1 teaspoon of fish sauce and a pinch of white pepper, then whisk well. ● In another bowl, mix the tapioca flour, cornflour and water.

❷ Pour the oil into a frying pan over medium to high heat, ensuring it covers the whole surface. ● Pour in the tapioca and cornflour mixture so that it covers the pan completely. ● Cook until the edges start to come away and a crispy layer is created.

❸ Add the egg mixture. ● When the mixture begins to set, break the omelette into large pieces using a wooden spatula, then stir to cook any parts that are still raw.

❹ When the omelette becomes slightly golden, add the oysters. ● Stir for 30 to 60 seconds, then add the coriander. ● Serve with white pepper and fish sauce (or chilli sauce).

包子家族

小吃

炸藕片
LOTUS ROOT CHIPS

MAKES AROUND 4 SERVINGS

INGREDIENTS

FRESH LOTUS ROOT ....2 TO 3
SICHUAN GROUND RED PEPPER ....⅓ TEASPOON
GARLIC POWDER ....⅓ TEASPOON
SALT...⅓ TEASPOON
OIL FOR FRYING

❶ Peel the lotus roots. ● Using a mandolin, finely slice the lotus roots and place them in cold water. ● Run the slices under water, drain and rinse them again to remove excess starch.

❷ Pat dry using paper towel. ● Heat the oil to 160°C (320°F). ● Take about 15 to 20 slices at a time and place them gently into the oil.

● Use tongs to separate the slices. ● Once the chips are nice and golden, remove and drain on paper towel to absorb excess oil.

❸ Sprinkle with the combined Sichuan red pepper, garlic powder and salt.

包子家族

粽子
ZONGZI

MAKES 12 PARCELS

INGREDIENTS

PORK BELLY	500 G (1 LB 2 OZ)
CHINESE FIVE SPICE	1 TEASPOON
GLUTINOUS RICE	600 G (3 CUPS)
MUNG BEANS	400 G (14 OZ)
SALT	2 TEASPOONS
VEGETABLE OIL	A DRIZZLE
DRIED SHRIMP	50 G (1¾ OZ)
SHAOXING WINE	1 TABLESPOON
SALTED DUCK EGG YOLKS	12
COOKED CHESTNUTS (OPTIONAL)	12

ASSEMBLY

BAMBOO LEAVES	24
TWINE	12 PIECES

❶ Cut the pork belly into 12 pieces, sprinkle on all sides with Chinese five spice and allow to rest overnight.

❷ Soak the glutinous rice and mung beans in two separate bowls of water for at least 8 hours (or overnight). ● Drain, then season with a little salt and a drizzle of oil.

❸ Rinse the dried shrimps and place them in the Shaoxing wine to rehydrate. ● Soak the bamboo leaves and twine in water.

❹ To assemble, form a cone with a bamboo leaf and add the ingredients in the following order: ⅓ tablespoon rice, 1 tablespoon mung beans, 1 piece pork, 1 egg yolk, 1 teaspoon dried shrimp, 1 chestnut. ● Cover with ⅓ tablespoon rice. ● Using another bamboo leaf, cover the exposed side of the zongzi, then fold it over the other parts of the cone until a triangle is formed. ● Secure with twine so that it does not unfold.

❺ Cook the zongzi in a pot with enough water to immerse them. Cover with baking paper or a tea towel so that everything is well submerged, then put the lid on. ● Bring to a boil and allow to simmer for 30 minutes, then turn off the heat and leave to cook, covered, for another 30 minutes. ● Repeat these steps again: cook for 30 minutes, then leave to stand, covered, for another 30 minutes.

❻ To serve, undo the leaves, then eat holding the zongzi in your hands or on a plate with chopsticks. If they are savoury, you can dip them in a little soy sauce while eating; if you have made a sweet filling, try dipping them in a little icing sugar.

小吃

包子家族

凉拌手撕鸡
SPICY CHICKEN SALAD

MAKES AROUND 2 SERVINGS

INGREDIENTS
CHICKEN BREAST...1 TO 2
WATER...1.5 LITRES (6 CUPS)
GINGER...3 SLICES
CHOPPED RED ASIAN SHALLOT 1

SALAD
CUCUMBER ....½
CELERY ....1 STICK
SPRING ONION... 2 STEMS
CORIANDER...½ BUNCH
LETTUCE 1

DRESSING
LIGHT SOY SAUCE ....1 TABLESPOON
RICE VINEGAR ....1 TABLESPOON
SESAME PASTE.................................2 TABLESPOONS
SESAME OIL ....1 TEASPOON
CHILLI OIL ....1 TABLESPOON
+ A LITTLE TO GARNISH
WHITE (GRANULATED) SUGAR ....1 TABLESPOON

GARNISH
SESAME SEEDS

❶ Allow the chicken breast to come up to room temperature. ● In a large saucepan, boil the water with the ginger and chopped shallot, then add the chicken. ● Cook over medium heat for 8 minutes then turn off the heat and cook, covered, for about 15 minutes, until the chicken is fully cooked. ● Drain it and allow to cool.

❷ When the chicken is completely cold, cut it into strips.

❸ Cut the cucumber, celery and spring onion into thin matchsticks. ● Remove the leaves from the coriander stems. ● Wash the lettuce and separate the leaves.

❹ Combine all the dressing ingredients in a small bowl. ● Add the dressing to the chicken and salad and mix together. ● Serve with a drizzle of chilli oil and sesame seeds.

包子家族

小吃

凉拌猪皮
PORK RIND SALAD

CHINESE CUISINE EMPHASISES USING THE ENTIRE PRODUCT,
REDUCING WASTE AND EMBRACING TEXTURES. THIS RECIPE IS OFTEN MADE
AS THE STAFF MEAL WHEN PORK RIND IS LEFT AFTER THE MISE EN PLACE,
BUT THE DRESSING ALSO GOES WELL WITH PIGS EARS OR EVEN COLD NOODLES.

MAKES AROUND 2 SERVINGS

INGREDIENTS

PORK RIND .... 300 G (10½ OZ)
CHOPPED GINGER .... 30 G (1 OZ)
THINLY SLICED GARLIC .... 30 G (1 OZ)
SHAOXING WINE .... 2 TABLESPOONS
SOY SAUCE .... 2 TABLESPOONS

WHITE (GRANULATED) SUGAR .... ½ TABLESPOON
BLACK VINEGAR .... 4 TEASPOONS
DRIED CHILLI .... 1 TEASPOON
CHOPPED SPRING ONION .... 1 STEM
SHAOXING WINE .... 2 TABLESPOONS
SESAME OIL .... 4 TEASPOONS
SALT .... ½ TEASPOON

DRESSING

MINCED GINGER .... 15 G (½ OZ)
MINCED GARLIC .... 5 G (⅛ OZ)
SPICY BEAN PASTE (DOUBANJIANG) .... 1 TEASPOON

GARNISH
YOUR CHOICE OF SPRING ONION, CORIANDER,
MINT, THAI BASIL ETC.

❶ Place the pork rind in a saucepan with cold water, cover and bring to a boil. ● Discard the water. ● Fill the pan with water again and add the chopped ginger, thinly sliced garlic, Shaoxing wine and soy sauce. ● Bring to a boil and simmer for 1 hour. ● Remove the rind from the liquid and allow to cool completely, then slice.

❷ Mix all the dressing ingredients with the pork strips and serve with finely chopped spring onion or fresh herbs.

包子家族

皮蛋豆腐
TOFU AND CENTURY EGG

MAKES AROUND 2 SERVINGS

INGREDIENTS

CENTURY EGG	1
SILKEN TOFU	250 G (9 OZ)

SAUCE

CORIANDER	8 STEMS
LIGHT SOY SAUCE	90 ML (3 FL OZ)
BLACK VINEGAR	25 ML (¾ FL OZ)
SESAME OIL	25 ML (¾ FL OZ)
WHITE (GRANULATED) SUGAR	3 TEASPOONS
FRESH RED CHILLI	½ (TO YOUR TASTE)

TO SERVE

FRIED SHALLOTS	1 TABLESPOON
DRIED PORK	1 SMALL HANDFUL
CHOPPED SPRING ONION	1 TABLESPOON
FRESH RED CHILLI	½

❶ Finely chop the coriander stems (set aside 4 or 5 leaves and 1 teaspoon of sliced stems to garnish). ● Mix all the sauce ingredients in a jar and shake vigorously. ● Set aside for at least 1 hour.

❷ Peel the egg and cut it into eighths. ● Drain the tofu and carefully place it on the serving plate. ● Put the fried shallots on the tofu, which will add texture for the egg pieces to stick to. ● Place a few egg pieces on the tofu and arrange the rest around it.

❸ Shake the sauce again, then pour it over the egg pieces and tofu. ● Garnish with a spoonful of chopped coriander, dried pork, chopped spring onion, coriander leaves and chopped fresh chilli.

包子
家族

包子和点心

BAO & DIM SUM

83

包子和点心

包子和点心的来源
HISTORY OF BAO AND DIM SUM

包子家族

Bao is something that is very close to our hearts. It is both simple to eat and to transport, but is also complex to make, requiring a certain expertise. In China, bao can be eaten anywhere, at any time of the day. Importantly, there is a distinction between bao and baozi. Baozi, which are steamed buns with filling, can be considered a bao, but bao is not necessarily a baozi. Xiao long bao, for example, are small steamed bites with a thin pastry that contains a filling and a broth. They are not considered to be baozi.

Dim sum in Mandarin is called 點心 *dian xin* and means 'touch the heart'. In Cantonese, going out to eat dim sum is called *yum cha,* which means 'drink tea'. These translations perfectly illustrate the essence of this practice, which consists of eating small dishes served with tea. They are small because they are more intended to touch the heart than to fill a stomach. Dim sum, as we know them today, are from Canton and began to emerge during the Silk Road era, when travellers would stop in tea houses to relax, drink tea and sometimes eat.

包子和点心

包子分解步骤
STEP-BY-STEP BAOZI

INGREDIENTS FOR 18 TO 20 BAOZI

BREAD FLOUR (T65)	500 G (3⅓ CUPS)
BAKING POWDER	1 TEASPOON
SALT	1 TEASPOON
WHITE (GRANULATED) SUGAR	75 G (2⅓ OZ)
INSTANT DRIED YEAST	5 G (⅛ OZ)
WARM WATER	250 ML (1 CUP)

❶ PREPARING THE DOUGH BY HAND
Put all the dry ingredients, except the yeast, into a large bowl. ● In another bowl, add warm water to the instant yeast and mix. ● Pour the water-yeast mixture onto the dry ingredients. ● Using a pair of chopsticks, gently mix in circular movements from the centre outwards, slowly combining the wet and dry ingredients until they are no longer wet to touch and form a large ball of dough, not smooth but that holds together. ● Remove excess dough from the chopsticks and add to the mixture. ● Place the dough on a flat, clean surface. ● Use the palms of your hands to knead the dough, incorporating the remaining flour in the bowl. ● If the ball is sticky after 1 minute of kneading, sprinkle lightly with flour during kneading. ● If the dough is too dry, wet your hands and continue kneading until the dough is no longer dry. ● Continue to knead the dough for 8 to 10 minutes, until the surface is smooth and the dough elastic (when you push a finger into the dough, it should return to its original shape).

包子家族

包子和点心

**❶ PREPARING THE DOUGH WITH
AN ELECTRIC MIXER**

Put all the ingredients into the stand mixer bowl using the dough hook attachment. ● Mix at slow speed for 10 minutes. ● Check the elasticity of the dough as well as its texture – it should be smooth. ● Continue mixing for another 1 to 2 minutes if necessary.

❷ LET THE DOUGH RISE

Remove the dough from the mixer bowl and place it in a large bowl covered with cling film, or a slightly damp and clean tea towel. ● Leave the dough to rest in a warm place until it doubles in volume. ● The time may vary depending on the conditions in your kitchen. ● At 35°C (95°F) with some humidity, it can take as little as 15 to 20 minutes; at 21°C (70°F) with dry air, it can take much longer. ● Use dough size as a guide, rather than time.

❸ KNOCK DOWN THE DOUGH

Take the dough out of its bowl and place it on a lightly floured surface. ● Knead the dough, taking care to remove large air pockets. ● As you knead, you may find that it becomes easier as the air bubbles become smaller and evenly distributed throughout the dough. ● If you cut the dough and see a lot of bubbles, continue kneading until they are barely visible.

❹ PORTION THE DOUGH

Cut the dough in half and roll into logs with roughly the circumference of an apricot. Using a cookie cutter or a straight knife, cut the dough into 50 g (1¾ oz) pieces. ● Lightly sprinkle the dough pieces with flour and move them around so that they are lightly coated with flour. ● Use only enough flour so that the pieces do not stick to each other or to the work surface, as using too much flour will make the dough less shiny once steamed. ● Take each piece of dough and flatten it with the base of your hand, with the less attractive side facing up.

包子家族

包子和点心

包子分解 步驟
STEP-BY-STEP BAOZI

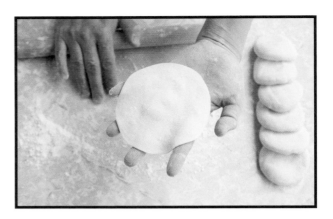

❺ ROLL OUT ROUNDS

Place a wooden rolling pin under the palm of your dominant hand. ● Start from the bottom of the dough circle and roll upwards with medium pressure, almost to the centre of the dough, then roll back towards yourself. ● Using your other hand, rotate the dough 30 degrees and repeat. ● Keep turning and rolling until you have rolled the entire round. ● The centre of the dough should be slightly raised – the thickness helps prevent the baozi from overflowing and balances the amount of dough around the filling. ● The edges of the dough should be thinner so that the dough is not too thick at the top after folding the baozi. ● You can roll a second time to even out the shape and thickness. ● In general, if the filling is runnier or separates easily, the circle should be larger.

❻ ADD THE FILLING AND ASSEMBLE

Place a round of dough in the palm of your hand. ● Using a spoon, add 35 to 40 g (1¼ to 1½ oz) filling to the centre of the dough and make a hollow with your hand so that the dough and filling are well-supported. ● With the index finger and thumb of your other hand, make a 'pinch' shape pointing downwards. ● Make a fold along the edge of the dough round and pinch gently. ● Repeat the process, rotating in the same direction. ● You have to pinch each time with one hand, and slowly turn the base of the dough with your other hand. ● You can use the thumb of the hand holding the baozi to push the filling in if it starts to come out.

包子家族

● Continue until you can see less and less of the filling and the baozi is completely sealed. ● If you need to, pinch the top seal several times to ensure it is fully closed and to prevent the baozi from exploding during cooking. ● Place each baozi in a steamer basket on squares of baking paper or on a baking tray lined with baking paper, leaving at least 3 cm (1¼ inches) between each baozi to allow them to expand.

❼ LET THE BAOZI RISE

Baozi dough will have to rise once more before cooking. ● As with the initial rising, the time it takes will depend on the temperature and humidity of the room.

Where and how to let it rise? In an oven with 100% humidity at 37°C (99°F) for 5 minutes. ● In a covered steamer basket over hot water (with heat off) for 10 to 15 minutes. ● In a normal oven preheated to the lowest temperature, then turned off with the door ajar. After 5 minutes, the air inside the oven should be warm when you put your hand in. Place the baozi inside and leave them to rest for 5 minutes with the oven door still ajar. ● The result needs to be a dough that is less dense than after assembling the baozi, and that is soft to touch. In terms of size, they should become slightly larger.

Errors to avoid during this step:
● Allowing the dough to rise in a draughty place. This will cause the surface to dry out and crack as the dough rises. ● Allowing too much rising time, and therefore too much fermentation. This will cause the baozi to lose its shape and even open once it is cooked.

❽ STEAMING

If you choose to steam in bamboo baskets, carefully arrange the baozi before turning on the heat to avoid burning yourself with the steam. ● If you are steaming in an oven, set the oven to 100°C (200°F) at full humidity. ● Steam for 12 minutes for baozi with a pre-cooked filling and 15 minutes if the filling is raw. ● Turn off the heat and allow to stand for 2 minutes before opening the lid of the steamer basket or the oven door. ● Bon appetit!

包子和点心

包子家族

包
子
和
点
心

蔬菜包子
VEGETARIAN BAOZI

MAKES AROUND 18 TO 20 BAOZI

INGREDIENTS

STAR ANISE	1
CINNAMON STICK	1
VEGETABLE OIL	80 ML (⅓ CUP)
SICHUAN GROUND RED PEPPER	1 TEASPOON
DRIED BLACK MUSHROOMS	100 G (3½ OZ)
SWEET POTATO VERMICELLI	100 G (3½ OZ)
GREEN CABBAGE	300 G (10½ OZ)
CARROTS	200 G (7 OZ)
CHOPPED SPRING ONION	2 STEMS
CHOPPED GARLIC	1 TABLESPOON
CHOPPED GINGER	1 TABLESPOON
OYSTER SAUCE	2 TABLESPOONS
SALT	
BAOZI DOUGH (PAGE 86)	

❶ Combine the star anise, cinnamon, oil and Sichuan pepper in a small saucepan and then heat until it reaches 120°C (250°F). ● The aim is not to fry but to infuse the oil with the spices and bring out the fragrances.

❷ Rehydrate the black mushrooms and vermicelli in water, then chop finely. ● Chop the cabbage and carrots, add salt to draw out excess water from the vegetables and allow to stand for about 30 minutes. ● After squeezing water from the vegetables, add the black mushrooms, vermicelli, chopped spring onion, garlic and ginger, then mix. ● Add the infused oil and oyster sauce. ● Mix again. ● You can make this recipe 100% vegetarian by replacing the oyster sauce with a mushroom-based version.

❸ Assemble according to the step-by-step instructions on pages 86–89. ● Each baozi should contain 50 g (1¾ oz) dough and 40 g (1½ oz) filling. ● Let the baozi rise for the second time in a warm, humid place for 20 minutes. ● Steam for 14 minutes and serve immediately.

包
子
家
族

包子和点心

猪肉包子
PORK BAOZI

MAKES AROUND 18 TO 20 BAOZI

INGREDIENTS

PORK MINCE	500 G (1 LB 2 OZ)
COOLED PORK BROTH	200 ML (7 FL OZ)
GINGER	10 G (¼ OZ)
LIGHT SOY SAUCE	2 TEASPOONS
DARK SOY SAUCE	2 TEASPOONS
SESAME OIL	1 TABLESPOON
VEGETABLE OIL	1 TABLESPOON
SALT	2 TEASPOONS
CHOPPED SPRING ONION	40 G (1½ OZ)
BAOZI DOUGH (PAGE 86)	

❶ Mix the pork mince and cooled pork broth together in a bowl until they are well combined. ● Peel and chop the ginger. ● Add the remaining ingredients except the spring onion. ● Once the mixture is well combined, add the chopped spring onion.

❷ Assemble according to the step-by-step instructions on pages 86–89. ● Each baozi should contain 50 g (1¾ oz) dough and 40 g (1½ oz) filling. ● Let the baozi rise for the second time in a warm, humid place for 20 minutes. ● Steam for 14 minutes and serve immediately.

包子家族

包子和点心

叉烧包
CHARSIU BAO

MAKES AROUND 18 TO 20 BAO

INGREDIENTS

CRUSHED GARLIC	30 G (1 OZ)
SLICED GINGER	30 G (1 OZ)
ROUGHLY CHOPPED SPRING ONION	30 G (1 OZ)
SHAOXING WINE	2 TABLESPOONS
SOY SAUCE	200 ML (7 FL OZ)
HOISIN SAUCE	150 ML (5 FL OZ)
RED FERMENTED BEAN CURD	100 G (3½ OZ)
WHITE (GRANULATED) SUGAR	100 G (3½ OZ)
WHITE PEPPER	2 PINCHES
PORK SHANK	450 G (1 LB)
HONEY	100 G (3½ OZ)
CORNFLOUR	30 G (¼ CUP)
WATER	60 ML (¼ CUP)
BAOZI DOUGH (PAGE 86)	

❶ Prepare the marinade by mixing all the ingredients in a bowl except the pork, honey, cornflour and water. ● Cut the pork into two large pieces, add to the bowl and leave to marinate for a minimum of 3 hours, or ideally overnight.

❷ Preheat the oven to 200°C (400°F). ● Drain the pork, reserving the marinade, then roast the pork in the oven for 15 minutes (on a rack if possible) to allow as much caramelisation as possible on the meat. ● Gently remove from the oven and brush with honey. ● Return to the oven for 15 to 20 minutes until the pork is slightly charred on the edges. ● Remove from the oven, leave to rest, then cut the pork into approximatley 1 cm (½ inch) cubes.

❸ Pour the marinade into a saucepan, bring to the boil, then simmer for about 20 minutes. ● Strain the liquid and simmer again. ● Mix the cornflour and water in a bowl, then pour the mixture into the hot marinade. ● Bring to the boil until the sauce thickens. ● Add the pork cubes and leave to cool.

❹ Assemble according to the step-by-step instructions on pages 86–89. ● Each bao should contain 50 g (1¾ oz) dough and 40 g (1½ oz) filling. ● Let the baozi rise for the second time in a warm, humid place for 20 minutes. ● Steam for 14 minutes and serve immediately.

包子家族

包子和点心

生煎包
SHENG JIAN BAO

MAKES AROUND 15 BAO

PORK RIND JELLY

PORK RIND	500 G (1 LB 2 OZ)
BOILING WATER	3 LITRES (12 CUPS)
CHOPPED SPRING ONION	10 G (¼ OZ)
SLICED GINGER	10 G (¼ OZ)

FILLING

CHOPPED GINGER	5 G (⅛ OZ)
SPRING ONION	5 G (⅛ OZ)
WARM WATER	200 ML (7 FL OZ)
PORK MINCE	150 G (5½ OZ)
SALT	1 TEASPOON
WHITE (GRANULATED) SUGAR	2 TEASPOONS
DARK SOY SAUCE	1 TEASPOON
LIGHT SOY SAUCE	1 TEASPOON

DOUGH

INSTANT DRIED YEAST	2 G (1⁄16 OZ)
BAKING POWDER	2 G (1⁄16 OZ)
BICARBONATE OF SODA	0.5 G (⅛ TEASPOON)
PLAIN FLOUR (T55 OR TYPE 0)	160 G (5¾ OZ)
WATER	80 ML (⅓ CUP)

OTHER

SUNFLOWER OIL	3 TABLESPOONS
WATER	100 ML (3½ FL OZ)
CHOPPED SPRING ONION	20 G (¾ OZ)
WHITE AND BLACK SESAME SEEDS	20 G (¾ OZ)

包子家族

包子和点心

PORK RIND JELLY PREPARATION

❶ Blanch the pork rind in boiling water for 5 minutes, then remove. ● Set the water aside. ❷ Cut the pork skin into small pieces and return them to the water. ● Add the chopped spring onion and sliced ginger, bring to a boil, then continue cooking over medium to low heat for 2 hours, uncovered. ❸ Stir occasionally so that nothing sticks to the bottom of the pan. ❹ Remove from the heat, strain everything and keep only the liquid. ❺ Pour the liquid into a container and refrigerate for 3 to 5 hours until it sets. ❻ Cut the jelly into small cubes.

FILLING PREPARATION

❶ Immerse the chopped ginger and spring onion in warm water and set aside for 1 hour so that the water infuses with the flavours. ● Strain and keep only the liquid. ❷ Mix the pork mince with salt and sugar first, then add the soy sauces. ● Mix well, then gradually add the infused ginger and spring onion water, until all the water is mixed into the filling. ❸ Knead the meat in the bowl three to four times so that the mixture is well combined. ❹ Add the jelly and mix well. ● The ratio must be 1:1. ❺ Refrigerate the filling for at least 30 minutes before you start assembling the bao.

DOUGH PREPARATION AND BAO ASSEMBLY

❶ Add the baker's yeast, baking powder and bicarbonate of soda to the flour and mix together well. ❷ Gradually add the water to the flour. ❸ Knead the dough for 5 minutes, then cover with cling film and allow to stand for 10 minutes. ● Knead again until the dough becomes smooth. ❹ Divide the dough into 15 to 20 g (½ to ¾ oz) portions. ● Make small balls. ❺ Roll out the dough to get a circle, then place a heaped spoonful of filling (about 20 g/¾ oz) in the centre. ❻ Bring all sides to the centre and fold to seal each bao.

COOKING THE BAO

❶ To cook the bao, add a little oil to a non-stick frying pan. ● Place the bao into the pan with the folds facing down, and leave a small space between each bao. ❷ Cook until the bottom of the bao is golden brown, then add water until it covers 1 to 2 cm (½ to ¾ inches) of the bao. ❸ Cover, then cook until all the water has evaporated. ❹ Remove the lid, then garnish with chopped spring onion and toasted sesame seeds. ● Serve hot.

包子家族

生煎包
SHENG JIAN BAO
page 98

包子和点心

燒賣解步驟
WRAPPING SIU MAI

❶ Use ready-made round wonton wrappers. Prepare the filling (see recipe on page 104).

❷ Place a wonton wrapper in the the palm of your hand. Put about 23 g (1 oz) filling in the centre.

❸ Bring the edges of the wrapper towards the centre by gathering them up to create folds all around the filling.

包子家族

❹ When the wrapper is properly adhered to the filling, flatten the base of the siu mai then, using the end of a spoon, press down on the filling so that it is well packed in and as much air as possible is removed.

包子和点心

烧卖
SIU MAI

MAKES AROUND 40 SIU MAI

INGREDIENTS	
WONTON WRAPPERS	**40**

FILLING	
DRIED SHIITAKE MUSHROOMS	**50 G (1¾ OZ)**
PEELED PRAWNS	**350 G (12 OZ)**
PORK SHANK	**450 G (1 LB)**
POTATO STARCH	**25 G (1 OZ)**

SALT	**8 G (¼ OZ)**
WATER	**50 ML (1¾ FLOZ)**
CHICKEN STOCK POWDER	**15 G (½ OZ)**
WHITE (GRANULATED) SUGAR	**20 G (¾ OZ)**
SESAME OIL	**1 TEASPOON**
VEGETABLE OIL	**1½ TABLESPOONS**
WHITE PEPPER	**¼ TEASPOON**
SALMON ROE OR REHYDRATED GOJI BERRIES	

❶ Prepare the filling: soak the dried shiitake mushrooms in water to rehydrate. ● Chop them finely. ● Cut the prawns roughly into chunks. ● Cut the pork shank into small 1 cm (½ inch) cubes. ● Add the potato starch, salt and water, then mix. ● Add the prawns and mix again. ● Lastly, add the shiitake mushrooms and remaining ingredients, mix again and refrigerate for at least 3 hours.

❷ For each wonton wrapper, place 23 g (1 oz) filling in the centre and fold, as shown in the step-by-steps on pages 102–103.

❸ Arrange four siu mai in each small bamboo basket that you have, so that they touch lightly. ● Being close together allows them to better retain their shape during cooking.

❹ Steam for 4 minutes. ● Garnish with salmon roe or rehydrated goji berries and serve immediately.

OUR TIP

Wonton wrappers can be found in all Asian grocery stores.

包子家族

包子和点心

虾饺
HAR GOW

MAKES AROUND 25 HAR GOW

INGREDIENTS

FROZEN PEELED PRAWNS	450 G (1 LB)
POTATO STARCH	10 G (¼ OZ)
LYE WATER OR SODA WATER	1 TEASPOON
SALT	¼ TEASPOON

FILLING

PORK FAT	40 G (1½ OZ)
SALT	1 TEASPOON
POTATO STARCH	8 G (¼ OZ)
BAMBOO SHOOTS	50 G (1¾ OZ)

WHITE (GRANULATED) SUGAR	15 G (½ OZ)
WHITE PEPPER	¼ TEASPOON
CHICKEN STOCK POWDER	8 G (¼ OZ)
SESAME OIL	½ TEASPOON

DOUGH

WHEAT STARCH	100 G (3½ OZ)
POTATO STARCH	20 G (¾ OZ) + 80 G (2¾ OZ)
BOILING WATER	200 ML (7 FL OZ)
VEGETABLE OIL	7 ML (¼ FL OZ)

❶ Defrost, rinse and drain the prawns. ● Cut them roughly into chunks, then mix them with the potato starch and beat until the mixture becomes sticky. ● Add the lye water or soda water and salt, then marinate for 20 to 30 minutes.

❷ Wash the prawns and leave them to soak in water for about 45 minutes to 1 hour, changing the water regularly.

❸ Prepare the filling: cut the pork fat into small pieces, then fry until golden. ● Carefully drain and dry the prawns, then marinate them in the salt and potato starch.

❹ Cut the bamboo shoots into cubes, blanch them in boiling water, then let them cool before draining well. ● Sprinkle the bamboo shoots with sugar and white pepper, add the powdered chicken stock and sesame oil, then add the prawns. ● Pat and mix until the filling comes together. ● Set aside in the refrigerator.

❺ Prepare the dough: mix the wheat starch and 20 g potato starch in a bowl. ● Pour in the boiling water and stir quickly to form a cooked dough. ● Allow to stand for 5 minutes.

❻ Add the oil and mix. ● Add in 80 g potato starch and knead on the benchtop until a smooth dough is formed.

❼ Roll out the dough into a log about 2 to 3 cm (¾ to 1¼ inches) in diameter, then divide into 13 g (½ oz) portions.

❽ Lightly oil a wooden cutting board, making sure it is stable and placed on a flat surface (you can put a damp tea towel underneath to secure it). ● Using the blade of a Chinese cleaver, first press each piece of dough to flatten it, then press while turning clockwise until a semicircle forms. ● Repeat the same movements counter-clockwise to get a circle.

❾ Place 12 g (½ oz) filling onto the dough and fold. Steam on high heat for 3 minutes.

包子家族

包子和点心

餃子分解步驟
STEP-BY-STEP JIAOZI

INGREDIENTS FOR ABOUT 15 JIAOZI

DOUGH

PLAIN FLOUR	500 G (3⅓ CUPS)
WATER	200 ML (7 FL OZ)
SALT	1 TEASPOON

❶ Prepare the dough: mix flour, water and salt in a bowl and start kneading. ● Transfer the dough to a benchtop and continue to knead until you get a smooth dough. ● Cover and leave to rest at room temperature for 1 hour.

❷ Prepare the filling (see recipe page 110).

❸ Divide the dough into four pieces to form balls, then roll them into logs of the same length and diameter.

❹ Take 18 g (¾ oz) portions and roll each into a ball. ● Lightly flour each ball. ● Flatten each ball of dough with the palm of your hand. ● Use one hand to move the dough, and the other to use the rolling pin. ● Even pressure must be used over the lower part of the dough.

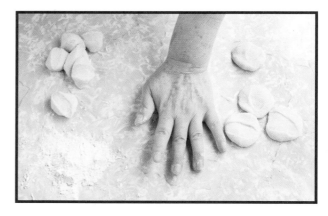

包子家族

包子和点心

❺ Rotate the dough and roll out gradually until you make a full turn. ● If the dough sticks to the bench-top, put the dough round directly into the flour, and then continue rolling out.

❻ When the dough is about 2 to 3 mm (⅛ inch) thick, place about 25 g (1 oz) filling in the centre.

❼ Using both hands, bring your fingers inward and squeeze the top of the dumpling with your fingertips and thumbs to close it.

❽ Steam or boil for 6 to 7 minutes. ● You can also cook them like guotie (see the pork and cabbage dumplings recipe, page 112): fry for 1 minute, pour in water, cover, and then remove the lid. ● Eat with black vinegar as a dipping sauce.

包子家族

包子和点心

餃子

JIAOZI

THIS RECIPE IS VERY POPULAR IN NORTHERN CHINA, WHERE YOU CAN FIND
MANY DIFFERENT FILLINGS AND COOKING METHODS (STEAMING, BOILING OR PAN-FRIED).
EVEN IF THE DOUGH MUST BE MADE BY HAND, THE FOLDING IS QUITE SIMPLE AND GIVES THE
JIAOZI ITS CHARACTERISTIC SHAPE, WHICH IS RECOGNISED BY DUMPLING LOVERS AROUND THE WORLD.

MAKES AROUND 40 JIAOZI

FILLING	
PORK MINCE	600 G (1 LB 5 OZ)
PORK BROTH	150 ML (5 FL OZ)
CHOPPED GARLIC CHIVES	150 G (5½ OZ)
EGG	1
OYSTER SAUCE	1 TABLESPOON
SESAME OIL	1 TEASPOON
CHOPPED GINGER	1 TABLESPOON
CHOPPED SPRING ONION	2 STEMS
WHITE PEPPER	3 PINCHES

❶ Prepare the filling: mix all the ingredients in a bowl, then allow to rest in the refrigerator for at least 20 minutes.

❷ To assemble, divide the dough into 18 g (¾ oz) portions. ● Roll them out using a rolling pin to obtain rounds the size of the palm of your hand. ● Add the filling to the centre of the dough and close on both sides using the thumbs and index fingers of each hand (see step-by-step pages 108–109).

❸ Steam or boil for 6 to 7 minutes, or cook in a frying pan: fry with a drizzle of oil for 1 minute, pour in water, cover, then uncover to get a crispy base. ● Serve with black vinegar.

包子家族

包子和点心

锅贴
PORK AND CABBAGE DUMPLINGS

MAKES AROUND 35 DUMPLINGS

INGREDIENTS
ROUND WONTON WRAPPERS .... 1 PACKET

FILLING
CHINESE CABBAGE .... 6 TO 7 LEAVES
PORK MINCE .... 600 G (1 LB 5 OZ)
PORK BROTH (OR CHICKEN STOCK) .... 150 ML (5 FL OZ)
LIGHT SOY SAUCE .... 1 TABLESPOON

SALT .... 2 PINCHES
WHITE (GRANULATED) SUGAR .... 2 PINCHES
WHITE PEPPER .... 1 PINCH
CHOPPED GINGER .... 1½ TABLESPOONS
SPRING ONION .... 2 STEMS
PEELED PRAWNS (OPTIONAL) .... 100 G (3½ OZ)
VEGETABLE OIL .... A DRIZZLE

❶ Prepare the filling: cut the Chinese cabbage into thin strips lengthways, then chop finely. ● Add some salt, mix and set aside in a colander for 20 minutes. ● Squeeze to extract excess water.

❷ Mix the pork mince with the broth, soy sauce, salt, sugar and white pepper in a bowl. ● Add the chopped ginger and spring onion, then mix again. ● Lastly, add the chopped cabbage to the mixture (at this stage, you can add chopped prawns to the filling, if desired) and mix well (to check seasoning, you can cook a small amount of filling in a frying pan).

❸ To assemble, put about 25 g (1 oz) filling in the centre of each wonton wrapper and close according to the step-by-step instructions on pages 108–109.

❹ Heat a frying pan (preferably non-stick) over medium to high heat and add enough vegetable oil to cover the surface. ● Add the dumplings one at a time next to each other until the pan is filled. ● Allow the underside of the dumplings to fry until lightly golden. ● Then pour in 60 ml (¼ cup) water, leave to cook covered over medium to low heat for 7 minutes. ● Remove the lid and continue cooking for 1 minute to get a crispy base. ● Transfer to a plate and serve with black vinegar.

包子家族

要抓

THE REAL WAY

BAO FAMILY 包子家庭

人心

TO THE
HEART

先抓

IS

THROUGH

BAO FAMILY 包子家庭

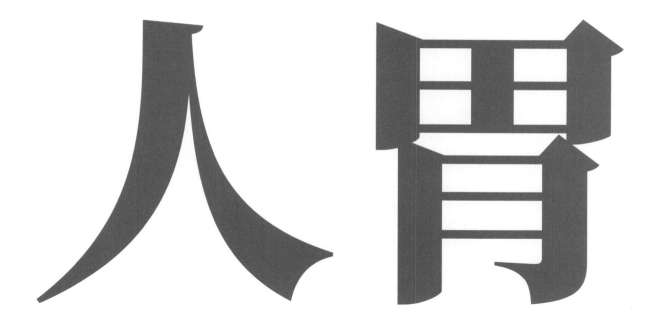

人胃

BAO FAMILY 包子家庭

THE STOMACH

包子和点心

萝卜糕
TURNIP CAKE

SERVES 2

INGREDIENTS

RICE FLOUR	110 G (3¾ OZ)
WHEAT STARCH	30 G (1 OZ)
CORNFLOUR	30 G (¼ CUP)
WATER	150 ML (5 FL OZ) + 440 ML (1¾ CUPS)
CHOPPED CHINESE SAUSAGE	60 G (2¼ OZ)
DRIED SHRIMP	20 G (¾ OZ)

VEGETABLE OIL	4 TEASPOONS
DAIKON (WHITE RADISH)	420 G (14¾ OZ)
WHITE (GRANULATED) SUGAR	1 TABLESPOON
SALT	1 TEASPOON
WHITE PEPPER	½ TEASPOON
CHOPPED SPRING ONION	10 G (¼ OZ)
SESAME CHILLI OIL	1 TEASPOON

❶ Mix the rice flour, wheat starch and cornflour with 150 ml (5 fl oz) water to make the breading.

❷ In a wok, sauté the chopped Chinese sausage and dried shrimp in a drizzle of vegetable oil.

❸ Cut the daikon into thin matchsticks, then cook in a saucepan over medium heat with 440 ml (1¾ cups) water until tender (about 5 to 10 minutes). ● Transfer the daikon to the wok and fry with the sausage and shrimp.

❹ Add the water and cornflour mixture and the sugar, salt and pepper to the wok, then stir until it thickens. ● Transfer to a rectangular dish and steam for 50 minutes (or until cooked). ● Leave to cool overnight in the refrigerator.

❺ Cut 4 to 5 cm (1½ to 2 inch) squares and brown them in a non-stick frying pan with a drizzle of vegetable oil. ● Repeat on the other side. ● Arrange three pieces of cake per plate and garnish with chopped spring onion. ● Serve with chilli oil.

包子家族

包子和点心

春卷
CHINESE SPRING ROLLS

MAKES AROUND 12 ROLLS

INGREDIENTS

CHINESE CABBAGE	400 G (14 OZ)
SALT	1 TEASPOON
COOKED CHICKEN BREAST	200 G (7 OZ)
GRATED CARROT	50 G (1¾ OZ)
SESAME OIL	2 TEASPOONS
LIGHT SOY SAUCE	2 TEASPOONS
WHITE (GRANULATED) SUGAR	1 TEASPOON
WORCESTERSHIRE SAUCE	TO YOUR TASTE
LARGE RECTANGULAR SPRING ROLL PASTRY SHEETS	12
OIL FOR FRYING	

❶ Cut the Chinese cabbage into thin strips lengthways, then chop finely. ● Add salt, mix and set aside in a colander for 20 minutes. ● Squeeze to extract excess water. ● Finely chop the chicken. ● Mix the chicken, cabbage and remaining ingredients, except for the pastry, together.

❷ During assembly, cover the rolls with a damp tea towel to prevent the pastry from drying out. ● To fold, place the spring roll sheets on the benchtop so that a corner is facing towards you. ● Put 40 g (1½ oz) filling in a line in the centre of the pastry sheet. ● Start folding the pastry sheet over the filling from the corner closest to you, rolling into a cigar shape. ● Halfway through, fold the sides into the middle, then continue rolling until a cigar is formed. ● Seal with a little water.

❸ Fry at 160°C (320°F) until the spring rolls are nicely golden. ● Serve with Worcestershire sauce.

包子家族

包子和点心

豆豉蒸排骨
STEAMED PORK RIBS WITH GARLIC AND BLACK BEANS

MAKES AROUND 10 SERVINGS

INGREDIENTS

PORK RIBS .... 300 G (10½ OZ)
FERMENTED BLACK BEANS .... 1 TABLESPOON
GARLIC .... 3 CLOVES
CORNFLOUR .... 1 TABLESPOON
LIGHT SOY SAUCE .... 1 TABLESPOON
SHAOXING WINE .... ½ TABLESPOON
VEGETABLE OIL .... 1 TEASPOON

SESAME OIL .... ½ TEASPOON
WHITE (GRANULATED) SUGAR .... 1 TEASPOON
SALT .... ½ TEASPOON
WHITE PEPPER .... ¼ TEASPOON

GARNISH

RED CHILLI, DESEEDED .... ½
SPRING ONION .... 1 STEM

❶ Cut the pork ribs into pieces. ● Soak in cold water for 30 minutes to remove excess blood. ● Drain.

❷ Rinse black beans with warm water to remove excess colour. ● Peel and chop the garlic.

❸ Coat the ribs with cornflour, then add the remaining ingredients.

❹ Leave to marinate for at least 1 hour.

❺ Place the ribs and marinade in a shallow dish that fits into your steamer. ● Arrange the ribs flat in a single layer. ● Steam for 13 minutes.

❻ Garnish with slices of red chilli and spring onion.

包子家族

包子和点心

马来糕
STEAMED SPONGE CAKE
MA LAI GAO

A STEAMED CAKE MADE WITH BROWN SUGAR THAT IS EATEN TOGETHER WITH DIM SUM.

MAKES APPROXIMATELY 4 PORTIONS

INGREDIENTS

MILK	60 ML (¼ CUP)
DARK BROWN SUGAR	180 G (6½ OZ)
EGGS	3
INSTANT DRIED YEAST	1 TEASPOON
PLAIN FLOUR	180 G (6½ OZ)
INSTANT CUSTARD POWDER	20 G (¾ OZ)
BICARBONATE OF SODA	½ TEASPOON
BAKING POWDER	1 TEASPOON
SALT	½ TEASPOON
VEGETABLE OIL	60 ML (¼ CUP)

❶ Combine the milk, sugar, eggs and yeast in a mixing bowl. ● Sift in the flour and pastry cream powder, then stir into the liquid mixture. ● Leave the batter to rest for at least 2 hours in a warm place until air bubbles appear.

❷ Meanwhile, cover a 20 cm (8 inch) diameter bamboo basket with baking paper, making sure all the edges are covered to prevent the batter from overflowing.

❸ Once risen, transfer 3 tablespoons of batter to a small bowl and mix it with the bicarbonate of soda, baking powder, salt and oil until a smooth mixture is formed. ● Combine this mixture with the rest of the batter and mix well.

❹ Pour the batter into the bamboo basket and steam for 40 minutes without lifting the lid.

包子家族

汤和面条

SOUPS & NOODLES 127

汤和面条

馄饨汤
WONTON SOUP

MAKES AROUND 4 SERVINGS

INGREDIENTS

CHICKEN CARCASS (OR WINGS)	1 KG (2 LB 4 OZ)
WATER	2.5 LITRES (10 CUPS)
GINGER	80 G (2¾ OZ)
SPRING ONION	3 STEMS
SALT	
WHITE PEPPER	3 PINCHES

SESAME OIL	1 TABLESPOON
EGG	1
CORNFLOUR + WATER MIXTURE	
(1:3 CORNFLOUR TO WATER RATIO)	1 TEASPOON
WONTONS (SEE FOLDING P. 168 AND FILLING P. 170)	20
SPINACH	200 G (7 OZ)

❶ Place the chicken into a Dutch oven or large casserole dish and cover with cold water. ● Bring to a boil, then discard the water to get rid of impurities. ● Fill the Dutch oven with water again and add the ginger and spring onion, cut into sticks. ● Bring to a boil, then cook over medium to low heat for 45 minutes. ● Strain the aromatics and add salt, white pepper and sesame oil to the broth to your taste.

❷ Pour the egg into the water and cornflour mixture in a bowl and beat vigorously. ● In a wok or non-stick frying pan, over medium to high heat, pour the egg mixture in to create a thin layer that covers the entire surface. ● Lower the heat and turn the omelette over once the edges begin to come away from the pan. ● Slice the omelette into thin strips.

❸ Add the wontons to the broth and cook until they float, then add the spinach and cook for another minute. ● Serve with spinach and egg strips.

OUR TIPS

To obtain a rich and tasty broth, it is best to use the bones, skin and meat of the chicken. If you use whole chicken wings, cut them in half to expose the meat and bone.

包子家族

(130)

汤和面条

台湾红烧牛肉面
TAIWANESE BEEF NOODLE SOUP

THIS RECIPE IS QUITE DETAILED – IT IS SUPPOSED TO TAKE A WHOLE DAY OR EVEN OVERNIGHT TO MAKE.
EACH ROUND OF INGREDIENTS ADDED TO THE POT SHOULD FILL YOUR HOME WITH TANTALISING SMELLS AND
AROMAS, WHICH WILL RESULT IN MELT-IN-THE-MOUTH BEEF AND SLURPS OF SATISFACTION. IT IS AN
ADVENTURE FOR THE SENSES THAT CULMINATES IN A SOUP THAT HAS BECOME A CELEBRATED DISH IN TAIWAN
AND IS MADE IN THOUSANDS OF DIFFERENT WAYS ACROSS THE PLANET.

MAKES AROUND 6 SERVINGS

INGREDIENTS

BEEF SHORT RIBS	1.5 KG (3 LB 5 OZ)
BEEF FLANK	500 G (1 LB 2 OZ)
SLICED WHITE ONION	1
GRATED GINGER	50 G (1¾ OZ)
CRUSHED GARLIC	5 CLOVES
ROUGHLY CHOPPED SPRING ONION	3 STEMS
ROUGHLY CHOPPED LEEK	1
SLICED CELERY WITH LEAVES	1 STEM
SLICED CARROT	1

SPICE MIXTURE

SICHUAN GROUND RED PEPPER	1 TEASPOON
FENNEL SEEDS	1 TEASPOON
CINNAMON STICK	1
STAR ANISE	1
DRIED LIQUORICE ROOT	1
DRIED ORANGE PEEL	1 PIECE
DRIED CHILLI	1
BAY LEAVES	2

SOUP

SPICY BEAN PASTE (DOUBANJIANG)	30 G (1 OZ)
SWEET FERMENTED BEAN SAUCE	30 G (1 OZ)
LAO GAN MA	15 G (½ OZ)
SHAOXING WINE	80 ML (⅓ CUP)
LIGHT SOY SAUCE	50 ML (1¾ FL OZ)
DARK SOY SAUCE	50 ML (1¾ FL OZ)

OTHER

ROCK SUGAR	50 G (1¾ OZ)
QUARTERED TOMATOES	2
WATER	4 TO 5 LITRES (16 TO 20 CUPS)
SALT	

GARNISH AND SERVING

FRESH WHEAT NOODLES	600 G (1 LB 5 OZ)
SMALL BOK CHOY	12
SLICED SPRING ONION	2 STEMS
CORIANDER	1 BUNCH
CHOPPED FRESH RED CHILLI	2

包子家族

汤和面条

❶ Sear the beef rib pieces in a deep pot until they are well browned on all sides. ● Remove the ribs and pour the beef fat into a Dutch oven or large casserole dish with around 6 litres (24 cups) capacity, leaving just a small layer at the bottom of the first dish, reserving the remaining fat. ● Place the beef flank in another saucepan and fill with water until covered by the equivalent of three thumb lengths of water. ● Bring the beef flank to a boil for 1 minute, then drain and set the meat aside.

❷ Over medium to high heat, heat the Dutch oven with the beef fat. ● Add the onion, ginger, garlic, spring onion and leek. ● When they begin to soften and brown, add the sliced celery and carrot cut into rounds. ● Continue stirring for another 2 to 3 minutes, then add the spice mixture. ● If necessary, add a little reserved beef fat so that the spices release their fragrances. ● Next add the doubanjiang, sweet fermented bean sauce (tianmianjiang) and Lao Gan Ma, then stir quickly. ● The thick sauces should only come into contact with the hot pan for a short time. ● Deglaze the Dutch oven with the combined wine and soy (do this gently if working over high heat such as on a gas burner). ● Let the mixture heat, then add the sugar, tomatoes, ribs and flank. ● Fill the pot with water, leaving a little room for it to simmer without boiling over.

❸ Bring to the boil, then simmer for 2½ to 3 hours, covered, skimming impurities and fat about every 20 minutes, until the beef has reached the desired tenderness. ● Turn off the heat and leave to cool for about 30 minutes. ● Using large tongs, remove the beef pieces carefully and place them in a container.

● Strain the soup into another container, squeezing the cooked vegetables to release their liquid. (You can throw away the vegetables as they have already released most of their flavour and nutrients, or you can keep them to eat with rice later, a fibre-rich meal lightly seasoned with delicious broth!) ● Allow the broth to rest and then skim the fat from the surface. ● Taste, and add salt if necessary to release the broth's different layers of flavour.

❹ At this stage, you can put the beef back into the soup, leave it to cool and keep it in the refrigerator. ● The flavours will continue to develop and be even better to eat the next day.

❺ Fill another deep pot with water and add 2 to 3 generous pinches of salt. ● If you have chosen thin noodles, add more salt to the water, as the noodles will take less time to cook. ● Cook the noodles according to the packet instructions. ● About 1 minute before the end of cooking, add the bok choy. ● Strain and divide the noodles and bok choy into large bowls. ● Pour hot beef soup over the noodles, making sure that each bowl contains some of both meats. ● Garnish with sliced spring onion, coriander and chopped chilli.

台湾红烧牛肉面
TAIWANESE BEEF NOODLE SOUP

page 130

汤
和
面
条

香菇炖鸡
STEWED CHICKEN WITH SHIITAKE MUSHROOMS

MAKES 6 SERVINGS

INGREDIENTS

WHOLE CHICKEN	1
LEEK	40 G (1½ OZ)
GINGER	8 G (¼ OZ)
GARLIC	15 G (½ OZ)
REHYDRATED SHIITAKE MUSHROOMS	300 G (10½ OZ)
	(40 G (1½ OZ) DEHYDRATED)
VEGETABLE OIL	A DRIZZLE
WHITE (GRANULATED) SUGAR	20 G (¾ OZ)
SHAOXING WINE	3 TABLESPOONS
STAR ANISE	1
BAY LEAF	1
FERMENTED YELLOW SOYBEAN PASTE	20 G (¾ OZ)
LIGHT SOY SAUCE	2 TABLESPOONS
DARK SOY SAUCE	2 TEASPOONS
SWEET POTATO VERMICELLI	150 G (5½ OZ)
SALT	3 TEASPOONS
CORNFLOUR + WATER MIXTURE (1:3 CORNFLOUR TO WATER RATIO)	4 TEASPOONS

❶ Cut the chicken into 10 pieces: thighs, drumsticks, wings, breasts and tenders. ● Cut the leek, ginger and garlic into small cubes. ● Rinse the mushrooms. ● Soak the chicken pieces in cold water to remove excess blood, then pat dry. ● You can keep the mushroom soaking water for cooking – it will add extra taste.

❷ Pour the oil into a Dutch oven or large casserole dish and caramelise the sugar. ● Before the caramel becomes too dark, add the chicken pieces, fry for 1 minute, then add the Shaoxing wine, leek, ginger and garlic, star anise, bay leaf and yellow soybean paste. ● Fry for 1 minute, then add the soy sauces (light and dark). ● Add the soaking water from the mushrooms (or plain water) until all the ingredients are covered. ● Bring to the boil, then simmer, covered, over low heat for 25 to 35 minutes, until the chicken is cooked.

❸ Add the mushrooms, vermicelli and salt and boil over medium heat for 12 minutes. ● Season and thicken with the cornflour and water mixture.

包
子
家
族

汤
和
面
条

玉米排骨汤
PORK AND CORN SOUP

THIS SOUP IS INCREDIBLY EASY TO MAKE, EXTREMELY COMFORTING IN ANY SEASON,
AND CAN BE ENJOYED PLAIN OR WITH NOODLES AND FRESH HERBS.

MAKES 6 SERVINGS

INGREDIENTS	
PORK MEAT AND BONES (RIBS/TRIMMINGS) ....800 G (1 LB 12 OZ)	**CORN ON THE COB** 2
	CARROT 1
	SALT OR FISH SAUCE

❶ Place the pork in a Dutch oven or large casserole dish. ● The pieces with bone and cartilage will give the broth an even richer and deeper flavour. ● Pour water into the pot until the meat is covered, bring to a boil, then turn off the heat.

❷ Once the pork is cooked, discard the water and keep the meat in the Dutch oven. ● Pour in water again to cover all the meat, bring to a boil, then simmer for 1 hour.

❸ Add the corn, cut into 1.5–2 cm (⅝–¾ inch) thick slices, and the carrot, cut into 2 cm (¾ inch) pieces, then simmer for 30 minutes or until the meat comes off the bone. ● Taste and add salt (or fish sauce) to your taste. ● Serve immediately.

包
子
家
族

汤
和
面
条

番茄蛋花汤
TOMATO AND EGG SOUP

MAKES 4 TO 6 SERVINGS

INGREDIENTS

TOMATOES	300 G (10½ OZ)
EGGS	3
MINCED GINGER	5 G (⅛ OZ)
CHOPPED SPRING ONION	10 G (¼ OZ)
WHITE (GRANULATED) SUGAR	10 G (¼ OZ)
WHITE VINEGAR	4 TEASPOONS
SHAOXING WINE	2 TEASPOONS
WATER	2 LITRES (8 CUPS) + 60 ML (¼ CUP)
CORNFLOUR	15 G (½ OZ)
SESAME OIL	1 TEASPOON
SALT	20 G (¾ OZ)
WHITE PEPPER	2 PINCHES

GARNISH

CHOPPED CORIANDER (OR SPRING ONION)	5 STEMS

❶ Roughly cut two tomatoes into eight pieces each and the remaining tomatoes into small 1 cm (½ inch) cubes. ⬤ Break the eggs into a bowl and whisk well.

❷ In a frying pan over medium to high heat, fry the large tomato pieces with the ginger, spring onion, sugar and white vinegar to bring out the aromas, then pour in the wine. ⬤ Add 2 litres (8 cups) of water and the remaining tomatoes, then bring to the boil for 5 minutes.

❸ Dilute the cornflour in 60 ml (¼ cup) water and gradually add it to the soup so that it thickens. ⬤ Slowly pour in the egg mixture, stirring the soup with chopsticks. ⬤ Season with oil, salt and pepper to your taste and garnish with coriander (or spring onion) to serve.

包
子
家
族

汤和面条

冬瓜排骨汤
WINTER MELON SOUP

MAKES 4 TO 6 SERVINGS

INGREDIENTS

DRIED SHRIMP	60 G (2¼ OZ)
WINTER MELON (WAX GOURD)	800 G (1 LB 12 OZ)
SICHUAN PEPPER OIL	1 TEASPOON
CHOPPED GINGER	20 G (¾ OZ)
SESAME OIL	2 TEASPOONS
SALT	25 G (1 OZ)
WHITE (GRANULATED) SUGAR	2 TEASPOONS
CORIANDER	15 G (½ OZ)
CHOPPED SPRING ONION	100 G (3½ OZ)
WATER	3 LITRES (12 CUPS)

❶ Soak the dried shrimp in cold water for 10 minutes. ● Peel and cut the winter melon into 5 mm (¼ inch) thick slices.

❷ Place all the ingredients into a Dutch oven or large casserole dish, reserving a little coriander and spring onion to garnish. ● Bring to a boil, then simmer until the melon is transparent. ● Season to your taste, garnish and serve immediately.

包子家族

汤
和
面
条

酸辣汤
HOT-AND-SOUR SOUP

MAKES 4 TO 6 SERVINGS

INGREDIENTS

PORK TENDERLOIN ....100 G (3½ OZ)
REHYDRATED SHIITAKE MUSHROOMS.................200 G (7 OZ)
                         (30 G (1 OZ) DEHYDRATED)
REHYDRATED BLACK FUNGUS.......................100 G (3½ OZ)
                         (20 G (¾ OZ) DEHYDRATED)
BAMBOO SHOOTS ....200 G (7 OZ)
TOFU ....200 G (7 OZ)
SPRING ONION.. 2 STEMS
GINGER...15 G (½ OZ)
VEGETABLE OIL ....A DRIZZLE
GARLIC ....10 G (¼ OZ)
LIGHT SOY SAUCE ....4 TEASPOONS
DARK SOY SAUCE ....2 TEASPOONS
WHITE (GRANULATED) SUGAR.................................20 G (¾ OZ)

CHINKIANG BLACK VINEGAR.........................3 TABLESPOONS
WHITE PEPPER ....1 TEASPOON
CORNFLOUR + WATER MIXTURE....................3 TABLESPOONS
(1:3 CORNFLOUR TO WATER RATIO)
EGGS 2
CORIANDER..3 STEMS
OIL FOR FRYING

MARINADE

EGG WHITE 1
CORNFLOUR ....1 TABLESPOON
SHAOXING WINE ....1 TABLESPOON
SALT...2 PINCHES
FRESHLY GROUND BLACK PEPPER...........................2 PINCHES

❶ Combine all the marinade ingredients. Marinate the pork for 20 to 30 minutes. ● Rinse and cut the shiitake mushrooms and black fungus into thin matchsticks. ● Cut the bamboo shoots, tofu, pork, spring onion and ginger into thin matchsticks. ● Fry the pork quickly in oil at 120°C (250°F).

❷ Pour a drizzle of oil into a deep Dutch oven or large casserole dish, then fry all the other ingredients cut into matchsticks and the chopped garlic. ● Deglaze with soy sauces (light and dark) and cover with water so that the water is 3 cm (1¼ inches) above the ingredients. ● Bring to a boil, then simmer over low heat for 20 minutes. ● Add the pork, sugar, vinegar and white pepper, and taste. ● The soup should be sour, spicy and salty. ● Adjust the seasoning if necessary with white pepper, vinegar and soy sauce (light) to your taste.

❸ Add two-thirds of the cornflour and water mixture and let it thicken. ● If the soup is still quite liquid, add the remaining one-third of the mixture. ● Beat the eggs in a bowl, then slowly pour into the soup to form long strands of egg by stirring with chopsticks using your other hand. ● Remove from the heat and serve with coriander.

包
子
家
族

主菜

MAINS
147

番茄炒蛋
TOMATO SCRAMBLED EGG

MAKES 2 SERVINGS, SERVED WITH RICE

INGREDIENTS

TOMATOES	3
EGGS	3
SALT	1 PINCH
VEGETABLE OIL	2 TABLESPOONS + A FEW DROPS
WHITE (GRANULATED) SUGAR	1 TABLESPOON
WATER	50 ML (1¾ FL OZ)
CORNFLOUR + WATER MIXTURE	1 TABLESPOON
(1:3 CORNFLOUR TO WATER RATIO)	

GARNISH

CHOPPED CORIANDER	2 STEMS
CHOPPED SPRING ONION	1 STEM

❶ Cut a cross in the base of the tomatoes and cook in boiling water for 30 seconds, then remove and peel the skin. ● Cut each tomato in half, then into quarters and divide each quarter into three pieces. ● Beat the eggs in a small bowl and season with salt.

❷ Pour 1½ tablespoons of oil into a frying pan over medium to high heat, covering the whole surface. ● Pour the eggs in so that they cover the entire surface of the pan. ● When the bottom begins to set, turn the omelette over. ● As soon as the other side begins to set, break into large pieces with a wooden spatula. ● Set aside on a plate.

❸ Pour ½ tablespoon of oil into the same pan and add the tomatoes, sugar, salt and water, then bring to a boil for 1 to 2 minutes. ● Add the cornflour and water mixture, simmer until the sauce thickens, then add the cooked eggs. ● Gently fry the eggs and tomatoes, remove from the heat and add a few drops of oil. ● Garnish with chopped coriander and/or chopped spring onion before serving.

核桃虾
WALNUT PRAWNS

MAKES AROUND 2 SERVINGS

INGREDIENTS

PRAWNS	500 G (1 LB 2 OZ)
RICE FLOUR	3 TABLESPOONS
CORNFLOUR	3 TABLESPOONS
CONDENSED MILK	60 ML (¼ CUP)
MAYONNAISE (SEE TIP)	60 G (2¼ OZ)
HONEY	30 G (1 OZ)
WALNUTS	150 G (5½ OZ)
WATER	2 TABLESPOONS
WHITE (GRANULATED) SUGAR	30 G (1 OZ)
OIL FOR FRYING	

❶ Peel and devein the prawns, keeping the tail. Slit the back of the prawn to remove the vein. ● In another bowl, mix the rice flour and cornflour. ● Combine the condensed milk, mayonnaise and honey in a mixing bowl.

❷ Fry the walnuts in oil at 160°C (320°F) for 2 to 3 minutes until golden, remove from the oil and set aside. ● Bring the water, sugar and walnuts to a boil in a small saucepan. ● Stir until there is no more liquid in the pan, then allow to cool. ● Once cooled, the sugar should be crystallised but not sticky.

❸ Coat each prawn with the dry ingredient mixture and fry in oil at 160°C (320°F) until the outside is golden brown. ● The frying time will depend on the size of the prawns, but it should take 1½ to 2 minutes on average. ● Place the prawns in the bowl containing the sauce and mix well until each one is coated. ● Add the nuts, stir again and serve.

OUR TIP

Kewpie mayonnaise is best for this recipe but you can use any other mayonnaise if you can't find it.

蒜蓉鱿鱼
GARLIC SQUID

MAKES AROUND 2 SERVINGS

INGREDIENTS	
SQUID	500 G (1 LB 2 OZ)
GARLIC	100 G (3½ OZ)
VEGETABLE OIL	200 ML (7 FL OZ)

OYSTER SAUCE	2 TEASPOONS
FISH SAUCE	1½ TEASPOONS
CHOPPED SPRING ONION	2 STEMS

❶ Score each squid with diagonal straight lines, leaving 2 mm (1⁄16 inch) between each cut. ● Do the same in the other direction to form a crisscross pattern. ● Blanch the squid in boiling water for 15 seconds.

❷ Chop the garlic and reserve 1 tablespoon. ● Fry the remaining garlic with all the oil except for a tablespoon in a frying pan over low heat. ● The garlic will start to foam slightly, releasing moisture. ● When it starts to brown, turn off the heat. ● If the garlic has become over-browned and turned black, discard it and try again. ● This step is key to achieving the correct result for this recipe – burnt garlic will result in a bitter taste.

❸ Pour the remaining oil into a wok over medium to high heat. ● Add the remaining 1 tablespoon of garlic, fry and pour in 1 tablespoon of the garlic oil (including fried garlic pieces). ● Over high heat, add the squid and stir-fry rapidly. ● Add the oyster sauce, fish sauce and chopped spring onion and stir again until the sauce is evenly distributed. ● Serve immediately with a drizzle more of garlic oil. ● The remaining garlic oil can be reserved in a jar, well covered, for 2 weeks.

红烧鱿鱼
HONGSHAO SQUID

MAKES AROUND 2 SERVINGS

INGREDIENTS

SQUID CUT INTO PIECES	500 G (1 LB 2 OZ)
COARSELY CHOPPED GINGER	1 PIECE
SHAOXING WINE	2 TABLESPOONS
CHOPPED SPRING ONION	5 STEMS
CHOPPED GARLIC	1 TEASPOON
CHOPPED GINGER	1 TEASPOON
VEGETABLE OIL	A DRIZZLE + A FEW DROPS
SPICY BEAN PASTE (DOUBANJIANG)	1 TEASPOON
RED CAPSICUM (PEPPER)	100 G (3½ OZ)
GREEN CAPSICUM (PEPPER)	100 G (3½ OZ)
RED ASIAN SHALLOTS	3
CORIANDER	3 LEAVES

SAUCE

SHAOXING WINE	2 TABLESPOONS
LIGHT SOY SAUCE	1 TEASPOON
DARK SOY SAUCE	A FEW DROPS
BLACK VINEGAR	½ TEASPOON
CORNFLOUR + WATER MIXTURE	2 TEASPOONS
(1:3 CORNFLOUR TO WATER RATIO)	

❶ Cook the squid pieces in boiling water with the coarsely chopped ginger, Shaoxing wine and a few spring onion pieces for 30 seconds to remove impurities. ● Drain and set aside.

❷ Prepare the sauce by mixing 1 teaspoon of Shaoxing wine, the soy sauces (light and dark), black vinegar and cornflour and water mixture.

❸ In a wok over medium to high heat, sauté the garlic and ginger in a drizzle of oil. ● Then add the doubanjiang, capsicums and shallots cut into thin matchsticks and fry for 1 minute. ● Add the squid and fry for 20 seconds. ● Pour in the sauce and stir for another 10 seconds (everything must happen very quickly so as not to overcook the squid).

❹ Add a few drops of oil to give the dish a glossy finish and garnish with coriander.

主菜

豉椒炒蜆
WOK-FRIED CLAMS

MAKES AROUND 2 SERVINGS

INGREDIENTS

CLAMS	300 G (10½ OZ)
SHAOXING WINE	1 TABLESPOON
LIGHT SOY SAUCE	1 TABLESPOON
WHITE (GRANULATED) SUGAR	1 TEASPOON
RED ASIAN SHALLOTS	2
WHITE PART OF SPRING ONION	30 G (1 OZ)
FRESH CHILLI	1
RED CAPSICUM (PEPPER)	100 G (3½ OZ)
CHOPPED GARLIC	⅔ TABLESPOON
CHOPPED GINGER	⅓ TABLESPOON
VEGETABLE OIL	1 TABLESPOON
SESAME OIL	A FEW DROPS
CHOPPED CORIANDER	2 STEMS
SALT	

❶ Soak the clams in salted water for at least 2 hours, then rub the shells well to remove any impurities. ● Rinse.

❷ Mix the Shaoxing wine, soy sauce and sugar in a bowl. ● Finely chop the shallots, the white part of the spring onions and the fresh chilli. ● Cut the red capsicum into thin matchsticks.

❸ In a wok over medium heat, sauté the garlic, ginger, spring onion, shallots, half the chilli and capsicum for 30 seconds in the vegetable oil. ● Add the clams. ● When the clams start to open, add the sauce and stir until they all open.

❹ Pour a few drops of sesame oil into the wok and serve with chopped coriander and the remaining fresh chilli.

包子家族

青口贝
WOK-FRIED MUSSELS

MAKES AROUND 2 SERVINGS

INGREDIENTS

MUSSELS	300 G (10½ OZ)
SPRING ONION	3 STEMS
GARLIC	1 CLOVE
SHAOXING WINE	1 TABLESPOON
LIGHT SOY SAUCE	1 TABLESPOON
WHITE VINEGAR	½ TABLESPOON
SPICY BEAN PASTE (DOUBANJIANG)	½ TABLESPOON
WHITE (GRANULATED) SUGAR	1 TABLESPOON
CHOPPED GINGER	1 TEASPOON
CORNFLOUR + WATER MIXTURE	1½ TABLESPOONS
(1:3 CORNFLOUR TO WATER RATIO)	
SESAME OIL	A FEW DROPS
CORIANDER	1 TO 2 STEMS
OIL FOR FRYING	

❶ Soak the mussels in salted water for at least 2 hours.

❷ Rub the shells well to remove all impurities and rinse.

❸ Cut the spring onion stems roughly into chunks, separating the white from the green. ● Finely chop the green part. ● Cut the garlic clove into 5 or 6 slices.

❹Mix the Shaoxing wine, soy sauce, white vinegar, doubanjiang and sugar in a bowl until the sugar is completely dissolved.

❺ In a wok over medium heat, stir-fry the garlic, ginger and spring onion chunks in oil for 30 seconds. ● Add the mussels. ● When the mussels start to open, add the sauce, then the cornflour and water mixture. ● Stir until the mussels all open.

❻ Pour a few drops of sesame oil into the wok and serve immediately with coriander.

主菜

如何正确使用筷子
HOW TO USE CHINESE CHOPSTICKS CORRECTLY

1

2

3

4

包子家族

1 Do not stick your chopsticks upright in your bowl! This reminds us of the incense sticks arranged near the offerings made to the deceased. Instead, place them next to or on the edge of your bowl. **2** Do not use your chopsticks to pass food to others. **3** Do not hit the dishes with your chopsticks because this implies begging for food and it is very impolite. **4** Don't cross your chopsticks over each other! Always place them side by side. **5** Do not use your chopsticks separately, and do not stick your chopsticks in your food in order to pick it up. **6** Do not leave your chopsticks in your mouth for a long time, or lick your chopsticks. It is very impolite and unhygienic since you use your own chopsticks to serve yourself from shared dishes. **7** Do not use your chopsticks to pull or bring a dish closer to yourself. **8** Do not point at someone with your chopsticks. It's just like pointing a finger and it's considered rude.

主菜

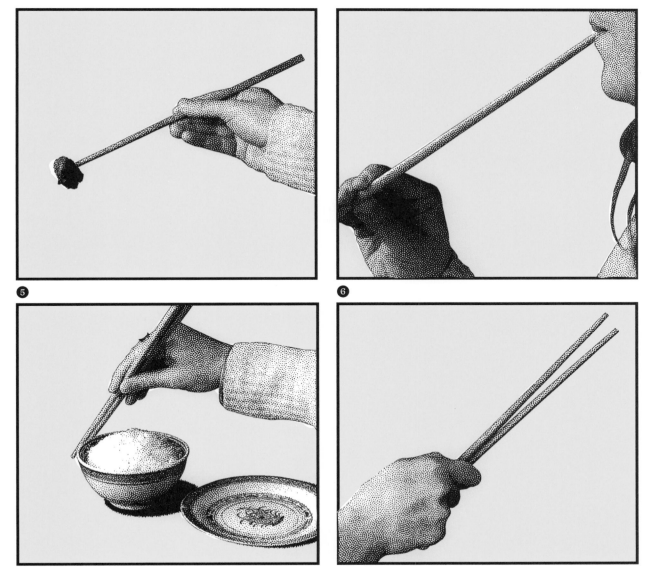

包子家族

清蒸鱼
STEAMED FISH

主菜

MAKES 4 SERVINGS

INGREDIENTS

WHOLE FISH (BASS OR SEA BREAM)	600 G (1 LB 5 OZ)
SHAOXING WINE	2 TABLESPOONS
VEGETABLE OIL	3 TABLESPOONS
GINGER	3 TO 4 SLICES
SPRING ONION	2 STEMS
SALT	

SAUCE

GINGER	1 PIECE
CRUSHED GARLIC	1 CLOVE
REHYDRATED SHIITAKE MUSHROOMS	3 TO 5

SPRING ONION	6 STEMS
VEGETABLE OIL	A DRIZZLE
WATER	400 ML (14 FL OZ)
WHITE (GRANULATED) SUGAR	2 TABLESPOONS
LIGHT SOY SAUCE	1 TABLESPOON
DARK SOY SAUCE	1 TABLESPOON

GARNISH

CARROT	½
LEEK, WHITE PART	1
GREEN CAPSICUM (PEPPER)	¼
VEGETABLE OIL	2 TABLESPOONS

❶ Prepare the sauce: peel and roughly cut the ginger into three pieces. ● Fry the peeled and crushed garlic clove, shiitake mushrooms, spring onion stems and ginger pieces in oil for about 1 minute. ● Once the mixture is fragrant, pour in the water, sugar and soy sauces (light and dark) and bring to a boil. ● Allow to simmer for about 10 minutes until the liquid reduces by half. ● Strain and set the sauce aside.

❷ Prepare the fish: make an incision in the belly and gut the fish. ● Rinse it under cold water, then pat dry with paper towel. ● Massage the whole fish with the Shaoxing wine and vegetable oil, then insert the ginger slices and spring onion stems into the belly. ● Salt lightly and allow to stand for 5 minutes.

❸ Steam the fish for 8 minutes (if the fish is large, cook for 10 minutes).

❹ Meanwhile, prepare the garnish – cut the carrot, leek and capsicum into thin matchsticks. ● Blanch them in boiling water for 1 minute.

❺ Heat the vegetable oil in a small saucepan over medium to high heat until slightly smoking.

❻ Once the fish is cooked, transfer it to a large serving dish and pour the sauce on the sides. ● Place the vegetables on the fish to garnish, then gently pour the warm oil onto the fish skin to add flavour to the dish.

包子家族

糖醋鱼
SWEET-AND-SOUR FISH

MAKES 4 SERVINGS

INGREDIENTS

WHOLE FISH (BASS OR SEA BREAM)	600 G (1 LB 5 OZ)
BEATEN EGGS	4
CORNFLOUR	50 G (1¾ OZ)
OIL FOR FRYING	

SAUCE

KETCHUP	3 TABLESPOONS
WHITE (GRANULATED) SUGAR	5 TABLESPOONS
RICE VINEGAR	100 ML (3½ FL OZ)
DRIED CHILLI FLAKES	1 TABLESPOON
FRESH PINEAPPLE	1
CORN KERNELS	15 G (½ OZ)
GREEN PEAS	15 G (½ OZ)
SALT	2 PINCHES

❶ Prepare the sauce: heat the ketchup, sugar, rice vinegar and chilli flakes in a saucepan over low heat, stirring occasionally to dissolve the sugar. ● Allow to reduce. ● Meanwhile, cut the pineapple into small pieces. ● Once the sauce has reduced slightly, add the pineapple, corn kernels and peas. ● Season with salt and set aside.

❷ Prepare the fish by cutting off the fins and removing the scales. ● Make an incision in the belly and gut the fish. ● Rinse it under cold water, then pat dry with paper towel. ● Cut off the head of the fish and set aside.

❸ Gently remove the backbone of the fish, making sure that the fillets remain attached to the tail. ● Using a pair of tweezers, remove the remaining bones and score (without piercing the skin) each fillet to create a crisscross pattern. ● Immerse the head and body of the fish in iced water to shrink the skin.

❹ Heat the oil to 180°C (350°F) in a wok or a frying pan big enough to hold the whole fish. ● While the oil is heating, dip the fish and head into the beaten egg, then the cornflour, making sure everything is well coated. ● Gently place the fish and head into the oil using a stainless steel skimmer to maintain the shape of the fish. ● Fry until nicely golden, then transfer to the serving platter of your choice.

❺ Warm the sauce over low heat and pour it over the fish.

主菜

馄饨解步骤
WONTON FOLDING

❶ Make the filling (see recipe page 170).

❷ Place a wonton wrapper in your hand with one corner facing up.

❸ Put 25 g (1 oz) filling in the centre of the dough, forming a rectangle spread out more along the length than the height.

包子家族

❹ Using the tip of your finger, draw a line of water along the wonton wrapper, just above the filling.

❺ Take the bottom of the wrapper and place it up to the water mark, then roll the filling upwards so that the filling is almost aligned with the top of the wrapper.

❻ Lightly wet one end of the wonton, then bring the other end back over by wrapping it around your fingers. Place the wet end on the other dry end and pinch until both are sealed together.

主菜

炸鲜虾馄饨
FRIED PRAWN WONTONS

MAKES AROUND 35 WONTONS

INGREDIENTS

PRAWNS	1 KG (2 LB 4 OZ)
FRESH LOTUS ROOTS	500 G (1 LB 2 OZ)
CHOPPED SPRING ONION	100 G (3½ OZ)
CHOPPED GINGER	25 G (1 OZ)
WHITE PEPPER	1 PINCH
LIGHT SOY SAUCE	60 ML (¼ CUP)
SHAOXING WINE	60 ML (¼ CUP)
SESAME OIL	2 TABLESPOONS
OIL FOR FRYING	

OTHER

WONTON WRAPPERS	35
CHILLI OIL	

❶ Peel the prawns and cut them into small pieces. ● Peel the lotus roots and use a food processor to crush them into tiny pieces. ● Mix the prawns and lotus root with the remaining ingredients.

❷ Fill and fold the wontons according to the folding instructions on pages 168–169. ● Wontons can be stored in the refrigerator for a maximum of 2 hours before cooking (to avoid the wonton wrappers becoming moist from the filling, which will cause them to stick together).

❸ Fry the wontons in oil at 160°C (320°F) until they are nicely golden. ● Serve with chilli oil.

包子家族

红油抄手
CHILLI OIL WONTONS

MAKES AROUND 35 WONTONS

INGREDIENTS

PRAWNS .... 1 KG (2 LB 4 OZ)
FRESH LOTUS ROOTS .... 500 G (1 LB 2 OZ)
CHOPPED SPRING ONION .... 100 G (3½ OZ)
CHOPPED GINGER .... 25 G (1 OZ)
WHITE PEPPER .... 1 PINCH
LIGHT SOY SAUCE .... 60 ML (¼ CUP)
SHAOXING WINE .... 60 ML (¼ CUP)
SESAME OIL .... 2 TABLESPOONS

OTHER

WONTON WRAPPERS 35
CHILLI OIL
HERBS OF YOUR CHOICE: SPRING ONION, CORIANDER,
MINT, THAI BASIL ETC.
SESAME SEEDS

❶ Peel the prawns and cut them into small pieces. ● Peel the lotus roots and use a food processor to crush them into tiny pieces. ● Mix the prawns and lotus root with the remaining ingredients.

❷ Fold the wontons according to the folding instructions on pages 168–169. ● Wontons can be stored in the refrigerator for a maximum of 2 hours before cooking (to avoid the wonton wrappers becoming moist from the filling, which will cause them to stick together).

❸ Cook the wontons in salted water for 5 minutes, then drain and transfer to a bowl or shallow plate. ● Pour chilli oil over the top and garnish with fresh herbs and sesame seeds.

包子家族

主菜

北京烤鸭
PEKING DUCK

MAKES 4 TO 6 SERVINGS

INGREDIENTS

WHOLE DUCK (GUTTED)	1
CRUSHED GINGER	30 G (1 OZ)
CHOPPED RED ASIAN SHALLOTS	2
CHOPPED SPRING ONION	1 STEM
CUCUMBER	1
LEEK, WHITE PART	1
HOISIN SAUCE	
STEAMED CHINESE BUNS OR PANCAKES	

MIXTURE FOR MASSAGING THE DUCK

HOISIN SAUCE	2 TABLESPOONS
CHINESE FIVE SPICE	5 G (⅛ OZ)
MINCED GINGER	10 G (¼ OZ)
CHOPPED GARLIC	10 G (¼ OZ)
SALT	1 TEASPOON

GLAZE

WATER	50 ML (1¾ FL OZ)
RICE VINEGAR	140 ML (4¾ FL OZ)
RED WINE VINEGAR	70 ML (2¼ FL OZ)
MALT SYRUP	2 TABLESPOONS

❶ Clean the duck and remove any remaining feathers. ● Boil a large pot of water. ● Use a hook or hold the duck by the neck above the boiling pot. ● Pour large ladlefuls of hot water onto the skin so that it begins to tighten. ● Repeat until all the duck skin is nice and tight.

❷ Make the mixture to massage the duck by combining all the ingredients. ● Rub the inside of the duck generously with the mixture, then place the crushed ginger, shallots and chopped spring onion inside as well. ● Sew the opening closed with a large needle and kitchen twine.

❸ Heat the glaze ingredients to dissolve the malt syrup. ● Brush the duck evenly with the glaze. ● Hang the duck to dry (use a fan if necessary). ● Once the skin is dry to the touch, the duck can be stored in the refrigerator overnight (uncovered), so that the skin dries out even further.

❹ Preheat the oven to 200°C (400°F) and place the rack at the lowest level of the oven. ● Put the duck into the oven with the breast facing upwards towards the grill. ● Roast for about 25 minutes, then lower the temperature to 180°C (350°F) and cook until the skin is crispy and the internal temperature reaches 80°C (175°F) (check with a meat thermometer inserted into the thickest part of the thigh). ● Remove the duck from the oven, slice and serve immediately.

❺ See pages 176–177 for how to slice and eat Peking duck. Slice the duck and serve immediately, with thinly sliced cucumber sticks, shredded white leek, hoisin sauce, and steamed Chinese buns or pancakes.

包子家族

北京烤鸭的正确吃法
HOW TO EAT PEKING DUCK

主菜

Peking duck is a typical dish from the city of Beijing. Originally it was a royal dish, which gradually became popular with everyone. The way the duck is cut is precise and very important. The crispy skin is cut into equal slices with a little fat and sometimes a little meat. In the traditional version it is the skin that is especially important, and it is not necessary to serve it with meat. We start with the back or the belly then move on to the thighs, placing everything on a plate as the duck is cut. At first, the skin that has been cut is served with pancakes, shredded leeks and cucumbers, as well as hoisin sauce. Then the meat is used to make a main dish that is usually wok-fried. For example a fried rice with pieces of duck or stir-fried broccoli with duck. Finally, the bones are used to make a broth to be served with the meal.

包子家族

主菜

海南鸡
HAINANESE CHICKEN RICE

MAKES AROUND 2 SERVINGS

INGREDIENTS

WHOLE SMALL CHICKEN	1
SESAME OIL	1 TABLESPOON

BROTH

GINGER	20 G (¾ OZ)
CHOPPED GARLIC	2 CLOVES
BAY LEAF	2
CHOPPED SPRING ONION	1 STEM
LEMONGRASS	1 STICK
SALT	½ TABLESPOON
WHITE (GRANULATED) SUGAR	1 TABLESPOON
WATER	2.5 LITRES (10 CUPS)

RICE

GARLIC	1 CLOVE
RED ASIAN SHALLOT	1
VEGETABLE OIL	2 TABLESPOONS
JASMINE RICE	280 G (10 OZ)
CHICKEN BROTH	500 ML (2 CUPS)

GINGER SAUCE

GINGER	2 TABLESPOONS
SALT	½ TEASPOON
CHINESE FIVE SPICE	1 SMALL PINCH
VEGETABLE OIL	3 TABLESPOONS

SWEET SOY SAUCE

LIGHT SOY SAUCE	3 TABLESPOONS
DARK SOY SAUCE	½ TABLESPOON
WHITE (GRANULATED) SUGAR	2 TABLESPOONS

CHILLI SAUCE

LONG RED CHILLIES	2
GARLIC	1 CLOVE
WHITE (GRANULATED) SUGAR	50 G (¼ CUP)
SALT	1 PINCH
RICE VINEGAR	100 ML (3½ FL OZ)

GARNISH

SLICED SPRING ONION	1 STEM
SLICED CORIANDER	2 STEMS
SLICED CUCUMBER	1

❶ In a saucepan, infuse all the broth aromatics (ginger, garlic, bay leaf, spring onion, lemongrass, salt, sugar) in water for 5 minutes, then place the whole chicken into this broth and bring to a boil. ● Allow to simmer over medium heat for 10 minutes, then leave covered for 20 minutes off the heat.

❷ Remove the chicken and immediately immerse it in a bowl of cold water to stop cooking and firm up the skin (keep the infused broth for cooking the rice).

❸ Once the chicken has cooled, transfer it to a serving dish or plate and brush the skin with sesame oil.

❹ Prepare the rice: chop the garlic and finely chop the shallot. ● Fry in a saucepan with a little oil. ● Add the rice and stir until each grain is coated with oil. ● Pour in the chicken broth and stir gently.

● Bring to a boil, then simmer, covered, over a low heat for about 15 minutes or until all the liquid has been absorbed.

❺ Prepare the ginger sauce: grate the ginger and mix it with the salt and Chinese five spice in a bowl. ● Heat the oil in a saucepan until it starts smoking. ● Pour gently over the ginger.

❻ Prepare the soy sauce: mix all the ingredients in a bowl until the sugar has dissolved completely.

❼ Prepare the chilli sauce: cut the chillies into 1 cm (½ inch) pieces. ● Blend with the other ingredients in a small food processor.

❽ Serve the chicken with the different sauces and garnish with sliced spring onion and coriander. ● Place the sliced cucumber rounds on a plate to accompany this dish.

包子家族

主菜

椒盐鸡肉
SALT-AND-PEPPER CHICKEN

MAKES AROUND 2 SERVINGS

INGREDIENTS

CHICKEN THIGHS	500 G (1 LB 2 OZ)
BEATEN EGG	1
RED CAPSICUM (PEPPER)	50 G (1¾ OZ)
GREEN CAPSICUM (PEPPER)	50 G (1¾ OZ)
VEGETABLE OIL	2 TABLESPOONS
CHOPPED GINGER	1 TEASPOON
CHOPPED GARLIC	2 TEASPOONS
DRIED CHILLI FLAKES	1 TEASPOON
FRIED GARLIC	1 TABLESPOON
SALT	1 TEASPOON
FRESHLY GROUND BLACK PEPPER	½ TEASPOON
CHOPPED SPRING ONION	1 STEM
OIL FOR FRYING	

BREADING

POTATO STARCH	100 G (3½ OZ)
PLAIN FLOUR	50 G (⅓ CUP)
GARLIC POWDER	25 G (1 OZ)
CHINESE FIVE SPICE	8 G (¼ OZ)

❶ Mix all the breading ingredients together and set aside.

❷ Cut the chicken into 25–30 g (1 oz) pieces, place in a large bowl with the beaten egg and mix.

❸ Cut the capsicums into thin matchsticks.

❹ Cover each piece of chicken with the breading and place on a dish. ● Fry a few pieces at a time in oil at 160°C (320°F) for 2 minutes, until the breading is golden brown. ● Continue until the chicken pieces are cooked.

❺ Heat a pan over medium to high heat and pour in the vegetable oil, add the ginger, garlic, capsicum and chilli flakes. ● Fry the capsicum until just cooked. ● Add the fried chicken, fried garlic, salt and freshly ground pepper. ● Garnish with chopped spring onion and serve.

包子家族

宫保鸡丁
KUNG PAO CHICKEN

MAKES AROUND 2 SERVINGS

INGREDIENTS

CHICKEN THIGHS	400 G (14 OZ)
SOY SAUCE	1 TABLESPOON
SHAOXING WINE	1 TABLESPOON
SALT	½ TEASPOON
WHITE (GRANULATED) SUGAR	1 TEASPOON
WATER	2 TABLESPOONS
CHINKIANG BLACK VINEGAR	1 TEASPOON
CHOPPED GARLIC	10 G (¼ OZ)
SPRING ONION	2 STEMS
DRIED WHOLE CHILLIES	2
CORNFLOUR + WATER MIXTURE	1 TABLESPOON
(1:3 CORNFLOUR TO WATER RATIO)	
PEANUTS	50 G (⅓ CUP)
SICHUAN PEPPER OIL	1 TEASPOON
OIL FOR FRYING	

MARINADE

SHAOXING WINE	1 TABLESPOON
RICE WINE VINEGAR	1 TEASPOON
LIGHT SOY SAUCE	2 TEASPOONS
WHITE (GRANULATED) SUGAR	1 TEASPOON
EGG WHITE	1
CORNFLOUR	½ TEASPOON
WATER	2 TEASPOONS
SALT	1 PINCH
WHITE PEPPER	1 PINCH
VEGETABLE OIL	2 TEASPOONS

❶ Cut the chicken into small approximately 1.5 cm (⅝ inch) pieces.

❷ Mix the marinade ingredients in a container, then add the chicken thighs and leave to marinate for at least 20 minutes.

❸ Fry the chicken pieces in oil at 120°C (250°F) until they are just cooked.

❹ Mix the soy sauce, Shaoxing wine, salt, sugar, water and black vinegar in a bowl.

● In a frying pan over medium to high heat, brown the chopped garlic, spring onion cut into chunks (set aside half) and the dried chillies cut into pieces in some oil. ● Add the chicken and stir for 30 seconds. ● Pour in the sauce, mix and then stir through the cornflour and water mixture until each piece of chicken is coated with sauce.

❺ Add the peanuts, remaining spring onion and Sichuan pepper oil, stir one last time and serve immediately.

湖南回锅肉
TWICE-COOKED HUNAN PORK

MAKES AROUND 2 SERVINGS

INGREDIENTS

PORK BELLY	500 G (1 LB 2 OZ)
GARLIC SCAPES	100 G (3½ OZ)
SPRING ONION	2 STEMS
LIGHT SOY SAUCE	50 ML (1¾ FL OZ)
SHAOXING WINE	50 ML (1¾ FL OZ)
VEGETABLE OIL	2 TABLESPOONS
SALT	1 TEASPOON
SPICY BEAN PASTE (DOUBANJIANG)	1 TEASPOON
RICE VINEGAR	2 TABLESPOONS
SWEET FERMENTED BEAN SAUCE	5 G (⅛ OZ)
FERMENTED BLACK BEANS	4 G (⅛ OZ)
SICHUAN GROUND RED PEPPER	2 G (⅟₁₆ OZ)
MINCED GARLIC	10 G (¼ OZ)
MINCED GINGER	20 G (¾ OZ)
CHOPPED FRESH GREEN CHILLIES	100 G (3½ OZ)
WHITE (GRANULATED) SUGAR	1 TEASPOON
CORIANDER	

❶ Start by removing the rind from the pork belly (it can be used for the pork rind salad, see recipe page 78) and cook the pork belly in boiling water for 25 to 30 minutes, or until fully cooked. ● Once cooked, cool in an iced water bath, then thinly slice into 2 mm (¹⁄₁₆ inch) thick slices. ● Cut the garlic scapes and spring onion into 5 cm (2 inch) chunks. ● Mix the soy sauce and the Shaoxing wine in a bowl and set aside.

❷ In a hot frying pan, brown the pork in 1 tablespoon of vegetable oil, season with salt then set aside. ● In the same frying pan, stir-fry the doubanjiang, rice vinegar, sweet bean sauce (tianmianjiang), fermented black beans and Sichuan pepper in the remaining oil for 30 seconds, then stir in the garlic and ginger. ● Fry, then add the garlic scapes, coarsely chopped green chilli and the spring onion. ● Stir-fry for 1 minute, then add the pork and sugar. ● Stir-fry again until everything is well coated. ● Garnish with coriander and serve.

主菜

红烧肉
HONGSHAO BRAISED PORK

MAKES AROUND 2 SERVINGS

INGREDIENTS

PORK BELLY .... 500 G (1 LB 2 OZ)
GINGER .... 7 SLICES
SHAOXING WINE .... 2 TABLESPOONS
SPRING ONION .... 3 TO 5 STEMS
VEGETABLE OIL .... 4 TABLESPOONS
ROCK SUGAR .... 50 G (1¾ OZ)
WATER .... 400 ML (14 FL OZ) + 1 TABLESPOON
STAR ANISE 1

BAY LEAVES 3
CINNAMON STICK .... ½
SICHUAN PEPPER OIL (OPTIONAL) .... 1 TEASPOON
SALT .... 1 TEASPOON
WHITE PEPPER .... ⅓ TEASPOON
LIGHT SOY SAUCE .... 1 TEASPOON
DARK SOY SAUCE .... ½ TEASPOON
CORNFLOUR + WATER MIXTURE .... 2 TEASPOONS
(1:3 CORNFLOUR TO WATER RATIO)

❶ Cut the pork belly into small 3 cm (1¼ inch) cubes, then cook them in 1.5 litres (6 cups) of boiling water with 2 slices of ginger and the Shaoxing wine. ● Skim off impurities occasionally, then remove the pork. ● Finely chop the spring onion, separating the white from the green.

❷ In a wok over medium to high heat, fry 3 slices of ginger in 1 tablespoon of vegetable oil. ● Add the pork and fry until golden, then set aside in a bowl.

❸ In the same wok, start making the caramel with the rock sugar, 1 tablespoon of oil and 1 tablespoon of water. ● Dissolve over low to medium heat until the mixture becomes golden, then pour in 400 ml (14 fl oz) hot water (the caramel should turn an amber colour).

❹ In a deep pot, fry 2 slices of ginger, the star anise, bay leaves, cinnamon, white part of the spring onion and Sichuan pepper oil in 2 tablespoons of vegetable oil, then add the pork and caramelised liquid. ● Season with salt and pepper and pour in the soy sauces, then simmer over low heat for at least 1 hour 30 minutes (if the pork is not completely covered at the start of cooking, add a little water).

❺ At the end of cooking, the meat should be tender and the sauce well reduced. ● Add the cornflour and water mixture and let it thicken for 1 minute. ● Serve and garnish with green spring onion.

包子家族

主菜

狮子头
LION'S HEAD STEWED MEATBALLS

MAKES AROUND 15 MEATBALLS

INGREDIENTS

CORNFLOUR	15 G (½ OZ)
	+ A LITTLE TO THICKEN THE SAUCE
WATER CHESTNUTS	130 G (4½ OZ)
SPRING ONION	3 STEMS
GINGER	10 G (¼ OZ)
GARLIC	10 G (¼ OZ)
PORK MINCE	500 G (1 LB 2 OZ)
EGG	1
SESAME OIL	1 TABLESPOON
WHITE PEPPER	2 PINCHES
OIL FOR FRYING	

SAUCE

SHAOXING WINE	80 ML (⅓ CUP)
OYSTER SAUCE	2 TABLESPOONS
LIGHT SOY SAUCE	1 TABLESPOON
WHITE (GRANULATED) SUGAR	30 G (1 OZ)
STAR ANISE	1
BAY LEAF	1
CRUSHED GARLIC	15 G (½ OZ)
WATER	150 ML (5 FL OZ)

❶ Bring all the sauce ingredients to a boil in a saucepan, then lower the heat and allow to reduce for 30 minutes until one-fifth of the original volume. ● Once the flavours are well balanced, strain the aromatics and add a little cornflour until the liquid thickens.

❷ Drain all the water from the chestnuts and chop them in a food processor. ● Finely chop the spring onion, ginger and garlic. ● Combine all the meatball ingredients (except cornflour) in a food processor and mix. ● Divide the mixture into 50 g (1¾ oz) portions. ● To form each meatball, throw it from one hand to the other, then roll it into a round shape. ● This movement removes excess air in the meatballs and forms nice round lion's heads.

❸ Coat the balls with cornflour and fry for 3 minutes in oil at 180°C (350°F). ● To finish, add the lion's heads to the sauce, then simmer until the meatballs are fully cooked.

包子家族

主菜

孜然牛肉
CUMIN BEEF

MAKES AROUND 2 SERVINGS

INGREDIENTS

BEEF (SIRLOIN OR RUMP STEAK)	250 G (9 OZ)
SALT	1 PINCH
SHAOXING WINE	1 TEASPOON
FISH SAUCE	2 TEASPOONS
WHITE PEPPER	1 TEASPOON
VEGETABLE OIL	4 TEASPOONS
CORNFLOUR	8 G (¼ OZ)
EGG WHITE	1
CHOPPED GINGER	1 TABLESPOON
CHOPPED GARLIC	1 TABLESPOON
CHOPPED FRESH CHILLIES	5

SPICY BEAN PASTE (DOUBANJIANG)	½ TABLESPOON
CUMIN SEEDS	1 TEASPOON
CORIANDER	½ STEM
SESAME SEEDS	1 TEASPOON
OIL FOR FRYING	

SAUCE

WHITE (GRANULATED) SUGAR	1 TEASPOON
BLACK VINEGAR	2 TEASPOONS
SHAOXING WINE	2 TEASPOONS
LIGHT SOY SAUCE	2 TEASPOONS
CORNFLOUR	8 G (¼ OZ)

❶ Thinly slice the beef against the grain of the meat. ● Combine the beef with the salt, wine, fish sauce, white pepper, oil, cornflour and egg white in a bowl and marinate for 15 minutes.

❷ Fry the beef in oil at 120–130°C (250–265°F) for 30 seconds, stirring gently until each piece is browned. ● Remove the beef, set the meat aside and reserve the oil.

❸ Prepare the sauce: mix the sugar, black vinegar, wine, soy sauce and cornflour in a small bowl.

❹ Pour a little of the beef frying oil into a frying pan over medium to high heat. ● Add the ginger, garlic, chilli and doubanjiang, then fry. ● Next add the beef and the sauce and stir for 10 seconds. ● Lastly, add the cumin seeds and coriander stem cut into 5 mm (¼ inch) pieces. ● Garnish with sesame seeds to serve.

包子家族

主菜

红烧茄子
HONGSHAO EGGPLANT

MAKES AROUND 2 SERVINGS, AS A SIDE

INGREDIENTS

LEBANESE EGGPLANTS (AUBERGINES)	250 G (9 OZ)
EGG	1
CORNFLOUR	1 TABLESPOON + 1 TEASPOON
LIGHT SOY SAUCE	1 TABLESPOON
DARK SOY SAUCE	1 TABLESPOON
SHAOXING WINE	1 TABLESPOON
WHITE (GRANULATED) SUGAR	2 TEASPOONS
WATER	1 TABLESPOON
CHOPPED GINGER	1 TEASPOON

CHOPPED GARLIC	1 TEASPOON
CHOPPED FRESH CHILLI	3 SMALL PIECES
SESAME OIL	1 TEASPOON
OIL FOR COOKING AND FRYING	

TO SERVE

CHOPPED SPRING ONION	10 G (¼ OZ)
CHOPPED FRESH CHILLI	½
TOASTED WHITE SESAME SEEDS	1 TEASPOON

❶ Cut the eggplants into approximately 2.5 cm (1 inch) thick pieces diagonally, then place in a very large bowl. ● Break the egg into a small bowl and beat well. ● Pour the egg over the eggplants and mix until they are all well coated. ● Then add 1 tablespoon of cornflour, stirring carefully until all surfaces are evenly coated.

❷ Fry the eggplants in vegetable oil at 160°C (320°F) until lightly browned. ● Eggplants should be deep-fried rather than pan-fried, so that a nice even crust is formed. ● Remove carefully and drain on paper towel to absorb excess oil.

❸ Mix the soy sauces, Shaoxing wine and sugar in a small bowl. ● Stir until the sugar has dissolved. ● Add 1 teaspoon of cornflour and 1 tablespoon of water to another bowl, and mix until there are no more lumps of cornflour.

❹ Heat a wok over medium to high heat and add 1 tablespoon of oil to coat the pan. ● Add the ginger and garlic, then stir for a few seconds.

❺ When they are fragrant but before they brown, add the soy sauce mixture and two or three small pieces of fresh chilli. ● When the wok starts to simmer, pour in the cornflour and water mixture, then bring to a boil until the sauce thickens slightly.

❻ Add the fried eggplant pieces and stir through the sauce until all the pieces are coated. ● Add the sesame oil and stir again, off the heat.

❼ Serve on a plate and garnish with spring onion, chilli and toasted sesame seeds.

包子家族

香菇炒上海青
BOK CHOY AND SHIITAKE MUSHROOM STIR-FRY

MAKES AROUND 2 SERVINGS, AS A SIDE

INGREDIENTS

BOK CHOY	500 G (1 LB 2 OZ)
BICARBONATE OF SODA	1 PINCH
REHYDRATED SHIITAKE MUSHROOMS	2
VEGETABLE OIL	1 TABLESPOON + A FEW DROPS
DARK SOY SAUCE	1 TEASPOON + 1 TABLESPOON
CHOPPED GARLIC	1 TEASPOON
SALT	1 PINCH
OYSTER SAUCE	1 TEASPOON
CORNFLOUR AND WATER MIXTURE	1 TABLESPOON
(1:3 CORNFLOUR TO WATER RATIO)	
SESAME SEEDS	1 PINCH

❶ Soak the bok choy in water together with the bicarbonate of soda (this will remove impurities that can be found at the root of the vegetable). ● Drain, then cut it into quarters lengthways (or six, if the vegetable is large). ● Thinly slice the shiitake mushrooms.

❷ Immerse the lower part of the bok choy in boiling water for 1 minute while holding the green leaves in your hand, then let it go completely into the water. ● Leave to cook for 1 minute 30 seconds to 2 minutes, then refresh in an iced water bath to stop it from cooking further.

❸ Pour the 1 tablespoon of oil into a frying pan over medium to high heat together with the shiitake mushrooms and 1 teaspoon of soy sauce. ● Stir for 1 minute, then add the garlic. ● Add the bok choy and fry for 30 seconds. ● Add the salt, oyster sauce, 1 tablespoon of dark soy sauce and the cornflour and water mixture.

❹ Cook until the sauce thickens, remove from the heat, then add a few drops of oil. ● Garnish with sesame seeds and serve immediately.

主菜

干煸四季豆
SICHUAN GREEN BEANS

THIS RECIPE IS TRADITIONALLY MADE WITH FLAT GREEN BEANS (OR ROMANO GREEN BEANS).
WE ADAPTED THE RECIPE TO USE FRENCH GREEN BEANS BECAUSE THE SEASON WAS PARTICULARLY ABUNDANT.
MAKE SURE YOU ADJUST THE COOKING TIME ACCORDING TO THE SIZE OF THE BEANS.

MAKES AROUND 2 SERVINGS, AS A SIDE

INGREDIENTS

GREEN BEANS ....500 G (1 LB 2 OZ)
PORK MINCE .... 60 G (2¼ OZ)
MINCED GINGER ....2 TEASPOONS
CHOPPED GARLIC..................................2 TEASPOONS
SICHUAN GROUND RED PEPPER ....1 TEASPOON

WHOLE DRIED CHILLIES..3
LIGHT SOY SAUCE......................................2 TABLESPOONS
WHITE (GRANULATED) SUGAR ....1 TEASPOON
BLACK VINEGAR ....1 TEASPOON
OIL FOR COOKING AND FRYING

❶ Fry the beans for 35 to 40 seconds in oil at 170°C (340°F), until they take on a slightly rough texture. ● Set aside.

❷ Pour a drizzle of oil into a hot frying pan, then add the pork mince. ● Fry until the meat is nicely browned. ● Add the ginger, garlic, pepper and chilli to the meat, then the green beans. ● Stir-fry quickly, pour in the soy sauce, sugar and black vinegar, stir again and serve immediately.

包子家族

主菜

豆芽炒韭菜
BEAN SPROUTS WITH GARLIC CHIVES

MAKES AROUND 2 SERVINGS, AS A SIDE

INGREDIENTS

BEAN SPROUTS	400 G (14 OZ)	GINGER	½ PIECE
GARLIC CHIVES	150 G (5½ OZ)	VEGETABLE OIL	A DRIZZLE
GARLIC	1 CLOVE	OYSTER SAUCE	1 TEASPOON
		SALT	1 PINCH

❶ After rinsing the bean sprouts and garlic chives, cut the chives into 5 cm (2 inches) pieces, then peel and chop the garlic and ginger.

❷ Heat the vegetable oil in a frying pan over medium to high heat and fry the garlic and chopped ginger. ● Before they start to brown, add the bean sprouts and stir-fry for 30 to 60 seconds. ● Add the garlic chives and stir-fry again for 30 seconds. ● Season with oyster sauce and salt. ● Stir-fry again for 30 to 60 seconds. ● Serve.

包子家族

主菜

清炒空心菜
STIR-FRIED WATER SPINACH

MAKES AROUND 2 SERVINGS, AS A SIDE

INGREDIENTS

WATER SPINACH...500 G (1 LB 2 OZ)
SLICED GARLIC .... 2 CLOVES

OYSTER SAUCE
(OR VEGETABLE STOCK + SOY) ....1 TABLESPOON
(OR 80 ML/⅓ CUP STOCK)

OIL FOR COOKING

❶ Rinse the water spinach well. ● Holding the stems together, cut the leaves, then divide the stems into chunks of around 8 to 10 cm (3¼ to 4 inches).

❷ Pour a drizzle of vegetable oil into a frying pan over medium to high heat and add the garlic. ● When the garlic releases its aromas, scatter the water spinach stems into the pan. ● After about 1 minute, stir the stems. ● Once the stems have started to soften (1 or 2 minutes later), add the leaves and oyster sauce. ● If you choose to use vegetable stock, add soy sauce to season to taste. ● Leave to cook and stir for 1 minute, until the leaves are tender. ● Serve immediately.

包子家族

蒜蓉炒芥兰
STIR-FRIED CHINESE BROCCOLI

MAKES AROUND 2 SERVINGS, AS A SIDE

INGREDIENTS

CHINESE BROCCOLI	500 G (1 LB 2 OZ)
RED CAPSICUM (PEPPER)	50 G (1¾ OZ)
VEGETABLE OIL	1 TABLESPOON
FINELY SLICED GARLIC	1 LARGE CLOVE
CHOPPED GINGER	1 TEASPOON
SALT	1 TEASPOON
WHITE (GRANULATED) SUGAR	½ TEASPOON
OYSTER SAUCE	1 TEASPOON
CORNFLOUR AND WATER MIXTURE	1 TABLESPOON
(1:3 CORNFLOUR TO WATER RATIO)	
SESAME OIL	A FEW DROPS
SHAOXING WINE	A FEW DROPS

❶ Peel the fibrous outer layer of the broccoli. ● Cut the broccoli into quarters lengthways. ● Cut the red capsicum into thin matchsticks.

❷ Cook the broccoli in salted boiling water until cooked but still crunchy. ● During cooking, prepare a bowl of iced water to refresh the broccoli and stop it from cooking further.

❸ Heat the vegetable oil in a frying pan over medium to high heat. ● Add the garlic and ginger. ● Once aromatic, add the broccoli and stir. ● Add the salt, sugar and capsicum. ● Stir-fry for 1 minute, then pour in the oyster sauce and the cornflour and water mixture.

❹ Once the sauce has thickened slightly and the broccoli is fully coated, pour in the sesame oil and Shaoxing wine, stir-fry one last time and serve.

VARIATION

To make a vegetarian version, remove the oyster sauce and add a little more sugar and salt instead.

炒士豆絲
STIR-FRIED SHREDDED POTATO
TU DOU SI

MAKES AROUND 2 SERVINGS, AS A SIDE

INGREDIENTS

POTATOES WITH FIRM FLESH	400 G (14 OZ)
GREEN AND RED CAPSICUM (PEPPER)	50 G (1¾ OZ)
VEGETABLE OIL	1½ TABLESPOONS
FINELY SLICED GARLIC	2 LARGE CLOVES
GINGER CUT INTO MATCHSTICKS	½ GARLIC QUANTITY
SALT	1 TEASPOON
OYSTER SAUCE	1 TEASPOON
WHITE (GRANULATED) SUGAR	1 TEASPOON
RICE VINEGAR	1 TABLESPOON
CHOPPED SPRING ONION	1 SMALL HANDFUL

❶ Wash and peel the potatoes. ● Cut the base of each potato so you have a flat surface to work with. ● Cut into approximately 1.5 mm (¹⁄₁₆ inch) slices. ● Spread the slices out by overlapping them slightly, then cut them into 1.5 mm (¹⁄₁₆ inch) thick strands. ● If the potatoes are very large, you can shorten the length to 6 cm (2½ inches). ● Immerse them in ice water and rinse until the water is clear. ● Soak in water at room temperature for 5 minutes, then drain. ● Cut the capsicum into thin matchsticks and put them in water to disgorge.

❷ Pour the oil into a hot frying pan. ● When it starts smoking, turn off the heat and fry the garlic and ginger until lightly golden. ● Add the potatoes immediately. ● Fry for 1 minute over medium to high heat.

❸ Add the salt, oyster sauce and capsicum and fry for 2 minutes. ● Lastly, add the sugar and rice vinegar. ● Fry until there is nearly no water left in the pan. ● The potatoes should be glossy but not browned. ● Garnish with chopped spring onion.

主菜

炒莲白
STIR-FRIED CABBAGE

MAKES AROUND 2 SERVINGS

INGREDIENTS

GREEN CABBAGE	300 G (10½ OZ)
CHOPPED GARLIC	1 TEASPOON
CHOPPED GINGER	1 TEASPOON
DRIED RED CHILLIES	3
SICHUAN RED PEPPERS	4 TO 5
VEGETABLE OIL	2 TABLESPOONS
WATER	100 ML (3½ FL OZ)
WHITE (GRANULATED) SUGAR	½ TEASPOON

SAUCE

SHAOXING WINE	2 TABLESPOONS
LIGHT SOY SAUCE	1 TABLESPOON
BLACK VINEGAR	1 TABLESPOON

❶ Roughly tear the cabbage leaves by hand. ● Prepare the sauce by mixing the Shaoxing wine, soy sauce and black vinegar in a bowl.

❷ In a wok over medium to high heat, stir-fry the garlic, ginger, dried chilli and Sichuan peppers in the oil until aromatic. ● Add the cabbage and stir for 1 minute. ● Pour in the sauce and water, then stir for 2 to 3 minutes until the cabbage starts to soften. ● Add the sugar and stir over high heat for 1 minute. ● Serve.

包子家族

韭菜炒鸡蛋
SCRAMBLED EGGS WITH GARLIC CHIVES

FOR THIS RECIPE NO ADDITIONAL SEASONING IS NEEDED – JUST ALLOW THE SUBTLE FLAVOURS
OF THE GARLIC CHIVES AND EGGS TO EXPLODE IN YOUR MOUTH.

MAKES AROUND 2 SERVINGS

INGREDIENTS

EGGS 4
SALT ....2 PINCHES
GROUND BLACK PEPPER ....1 PINCH

GARLIC CHIVES ....300 G (10½ OZ)
CORNFLOUR..1 PINCH
VEGETABLE OIL ....3 TABLESPOONS + A FEW DROPS

❶ Break the eggs into a bowl, add 1 pinch of salt and the ground pepper. ● Beat well.

❷ Trim the roots of the garlic chives, then cut them into 4 to 5 cm (1½ to 2 inch) pieces. ● Add 1 pinch of salt and the cornflour and mix gently.

❸ Pour the 2 tablespoons of oil into a frying pan over medium to high heat until it starts smoking. ● Lower the heat and immediately pour in the beaten eggs. ● Over high heat, stir so that the entire surface is covered with the egg. ● Gently unstick the omelette from the pan with a spatula if necessary. ● Once the omelette starts to brown, flip it over. ● Add 1 tablespoon of oil to the edges, continue stirring, and then flip it over again. ● Using a spatula, break the omelette into large pieces.

❹ Add the garlic chives and fry for 1 minute, stirring rapidly. ● The garlic chives will wilt and take on a bright green colour. ● Add a few drops of oil, mix, then serve.

主菜

麻婆豆腐
MAPO TOFU

MAKES AROUND 2 SERVINGS

INGREDIENTS

TOFU	500 G (1 LB 2 OZ)
VEGETABLE OIL	2 TABLESPOONS
PORK MINCE	100 G (3½ OZ)
MINCED GINGER	1 TEASPOON
MINCED GARLIC	1 TEASPOON
SICHUAN GROUND RED PEPPER	1 TEASPOON
CHILLI POWDER	1 TEASPOON
SPICY BEAN PASTE (DOUBANJIANG)	1 TABLESPOON
FERMENTED BLACK BEANS	½ TABLESPOON
SLICED FRESH RED CHILLI	1
DARK SOY SAUCE	½ TABLESPOON
WHITE (GRANULATED) SUGAR	½ TABLESPOON
WATER	50 ML (1¾ FL OZ)
CORNFLOUR AND WATER MIXTURE (1:3 CORNFLOUR TO WATER RATIO)	3 TABLESPOONS

❶ Cut the block of tofu into 2 cm (¾ inch) cubes and cook in salted boiling water for 1 minute. ● Drain.

❷ Pour 1 tablespoon of vegetable oil into a wok, add the pork mince and fry for about 1 minute until nicely browned (for a vegetarian recipe, you can replace the pork with shiitake mushrooms). ● Set aside the cooked pork.

❸ Add 1 tablespoon of vegetable oil to the same wok. ● Fry the following ingredients in this order, frying each one before adding the next: ginger and garlic, Sichuan red pepper, chilli powder, doubanjiang, fermented black beans, fresh chilli, dark soy sauce and finally the sugar. ● Fry until aromatic and the sauce turns slightly red. ● Once the sauce is smooth, add the pork and tofu and pour in the water.

❹ Simmer for 1 to 2 minutes, stirring the tofu cubes occasionally with the back of a spoon so as not to break them. ● Add the cornflour and water mixture, 1 tablespoon at a time, then let it thicken. ● Once all ingredients are well heated through, serve immediately.

包子家族

米饭和面条

RICE
& NOODLES
223

米饭和面条

广东炒饭
CANTONESE FRIED RICE

THERE ARE MANY WAYS TO MAKE FRIED RICE. THIS IS A LIGHT RECIPE THAT USES UP
LEFTOVER VEGETABLES, WHICH IN OUR CASE TURNED OUT TO BE LEEKS AND CHOY SUM STALKS.
YOU'LL GET A BETTER RESULT USING RICE WITH THE GRAINS ALREADY SEPARATED,
AND IDEALLY, RICE COOKED THE PREVIOUS DAY.

MAKES AROUND 2 SERVINGS

INGREDIENTS

EGGS	3
VEGETABLE OIL	120 ML (½ CUP)
CHOPPED GARLIC	2 TEASPOONS
CHOPPED GINGER	1 TEASPOON
SLICED LEEKS	150 G (5½ OZ)
LEFTOVER COOKED CHOY SUM	200 G (7 OZ)
COOKED RICE	400 G (14 OZ)
SALT	2 PINCHES
GROUND BLACK PEPPER	2 PINCHES
WHITE (GRANULATED) SUGAR	1 PINCH
DARK SOY SAUCE	2 TABLESPOONS
CHOPPED SPRING ONION	2 STEMS

❶ Beat the eggs in a bowl. ● Pour the oil into a hot frying pan. ● The ratio may seem high, but this will result in aerated eggs and flavoursome rice. ● Pour the eggs into the oil and stir. ● Cook for 20 seconds until the eggs are set, then add the garlic and ginger and stir again.

❷ Add the sliced leeks and fry for 1 minute, then add the leftover choy sum. ● Next add the rice and alternate stirring and allowing the rice to heat through. ● Finally, add the salt, pepper, sugar, dark soy sauce and a little spring onion. ● Stir over high heat so that all ingredients are well combined.

❸ Serve with the remaining fresh spring onion.

包子家族

米饭和面条

蔬菜炒面
STIR-FRIED VEGETARIAN NOODLES

MAKES AROUND 2 SERVINGS

INGREDIENTS

WHEAT NOODLES	250 G (9 OZ)
DRIED SHIITAKE MUSHROOMS	3
GARLIC SCAPES	2
BOK CHOY	2
MINCED GARLIC	2 TEASPOONS

CHOPPED GINGER	2 TEASPOONS
VEGETABLE OIL	2 TABLESPOONS
LIGHT SOY SAUCE	2 TABLESPOONS
DARK SOY SAUCE	3 TABLESPOONS
BEAN SPROUTS	60 G (½ CUP)

❶ Precook the noodles according to the packet instructions, then allow to cool. ● Rehydrate the shiitake mushrooms, reserving about 50 ml (1¾ fl oz) of the soaking water, then cut the mushrooms into strips. ● If the garlic scapes are thick, cook them in salted boiling water for 1 to 2 minutes (otherwise, add them directly to the noodles). ● Cut off the bok choy roots and separate the leaves.

❷ In a hot pan, fry the garlic, ginger and mushrooms in the oil. ● Stir for 30 seconds, then add the bok choy and garlic scapes. ● Mix again. ● Pour in soaking water from the shiitake mushrooms and cook for 30 seconds.

❸ Add the noodles, soy sauces (light and dark) and stir-fry energetically until all the sauce is well distributed and noodles are well heated through. ● Finally add the bean sprouts, stir-fry one last time and serve immediately.

包子家族

米饭和面条

干炒牛河
STIR-FRIED RICE NOODLES WITH BEEF HO FUN

MAKES AROUND 2 SERVINGS

INGREDIENTS

THICK RICE NOODLES	400 G (14 OZ)
BEEF	200 G (7 OZ)
ONION	½
SPRING ONION	30 G (1 OZ)
EGGS	2
OYSTER SAUCE	1 TABLESPOON
BEAN SPROUTS	100 G (3½ OZ)
DARK SOY SAUCE	1 TABLESPOON
OIL FOR COOKING	

MARINADE

DARK SOY SAUCE	1½ TABLESPOONS
LIGHT SOY SAUCE	¾ TABLESPOON
OYSTER SAUCE	1 TABLESPOON
VEGETABLE OIL	½ TEASPOON
WHITE PEPPER	1 PINCH
WHITE (GRANULATED) SUGAR	2 TEASPOONS
WATER	2 TEASPOONS

SAUCE

DARK SOY SAUCE	1½ TABLESPOONS
LIGHT SOY SAUCE	½ TABLESPOON
WHITE (GRANULATED) SUGAR	1 TABLESPOON

❶ Soak the rice noodles in hot water for 20 minutes (water should not be boiling).

❷ Meanwhile, prepare the marinade by mixing all the ingredients together in a large bowl. ● Thinly slice the beef against the grain of the meat, then add the meat to the marinade and leave to marinate for at least 15 minutes.

❸ Prepare the sauce by mixing the soy sauces and sugar together.

❹ Cut the onion into strips, roughly cut the spring onion into 5 cm (2 inch) chunks and beat the eggs in a bowl.

❺ In a hot oiled wok, first cook the eggs, then the noodles for about 2 minutes, until the texture begins to change. ● Next, add the oyster sauce and sauce ingredients, then stir for 30 seconds. ● Add the bean sprouts at the last minute and cook for 30 seconds. ● Transfer the noodles into bowls (or a serving dish).

❻ Add more oil to the wok, then brown the onion. ● Next add the beef, spring onion and dark soy sauce. Fry for 30 seconds until beef is cooked but tender.

❼ Serve on the bed of noodles.

包子家族

米饭和面条

葱油拌面
SHANGHAI NOODLES WITH SPRING ONION

ENOUGH SAUCE FOR AROUND 15 SERVINGS

INGREDIENTS

FRESH NOODLES ....150 G (5½ OZ) (PER SERVING)

SAUCE

SPRING ONION ....200 G (7 OZ)
VEGETABLE OIL ....300 ML (10½ FL OZ) + FOR FRYING
RED ASIAN SHALLOT ....90 G (3¼ OZ)
DRIED SHRIMP ....20 G (¾ OZ)
LIGHT SOY SAUCE ....90 ML (3 FL OZ)
DARK SOY SAUCE ....180 ML (¾ CUP)

WATER ....230 ML (7¾ FL OZ)
CORIANDER ....10 G (¼ OZ)
FINELY SLICED GINGER ....30 G (1 OZ)
FINELY CHOPPED CARROT ....150 G (5½ OZ)
WHITE (GRANULATED) SUGAR ....25 G (1 OZ)

GARNISH

SPRING ONION ....1 STEM

❶ Cut the spring onion stems, separating the white from the green, then fry them separately in oil until tender. ● Set aside. ● Cut the shallots into strips, fry them in the same oil, then set aside. ● Lastly, fry the dried shrimp in the same oil, drain the infused oil and set it aside (nothing is discarded).

❷ In a saucepan, bring to a boil the soy sauces (light and dark), water, coriander, ginger, carrot, half the fried shallots and half the fried shrimp, and simmer over medium heat for 20 minutes. ● Pass through a sieve, add the sugar and reduce until the desired consistency is reached.

❸ Add the 300 ml (10½ fl oz) oil to the slightly reduced sauce and bring just to the boil. ● Turn off the heat and add a little of the green part of the spring onion, along with the other half of the fried shrimp, then allow to cool (the sauce can be stored in the refrigerator for 1 week).

❹ Cook the noodles in salted boiling water until they are al dente (according to packet instructions). ● Heat about 70 to 80 ml (⅓ cup) sauce and stir it through the drained noodles along with the white parts of the spring onion.

❺ Garnish with the remaining fried shallots and green spring onion, as well as chopped fresh spring onion.

包子家族

米饭和面条

炸酱面
ZHAJIANG NOODLES

MAKES AROUND 2 SERVINGS

INGREDIENTS

PORK BELLY	100 G (3½ OZ)
VEGETABLE OIL	A DRIZZLE
CHOPPED GARLIC	1 TEASPOON
CHOPPED GINGER	1 TEASPOON
YELLOW SOYBEAN PASTE (HUANGDOUJIANG)	1 TABLESPOON
DRY YELLOW SOYBEAN PASTE (GANHUANGJIANG)	1 TABLESPOON

SWEET FERMENTED BEAN SAUCE (TIANMIANJIANG)	1½ TABLESPOONS
SHAOXING WINE	2 TABLESPOONS
WATER	200 ML (7 FL OZ)
FRESH NOODLES (WITHOUT EGGS)	250 G (9 OZ)
CARROT CUT INTO MATCHSTICKS	50 G (1¾ OZ)
EDAMAME BEANS SHELLED	50 G (1¾ OZ)
CUCUMBER CUT INTO MATCHSTICKS	50 G (1¾ OZ)

❶ Cut the pork belly into small cubes and fry in a wok with a drizzle of oil, garlic and ginger. ● Add the bean pastes and sauce and stir for 1 minute. ● Pour in the Shaoxing wine and water, then cook for about 7 minutes until it is reduced by half.

❷ Cook the noodles in salted boiling water according to the packet instructions, then add the carrot and edamame 1 minute before the noodles have finished cooking. ● Transfer immediately to a bowl of iced water to refresh and stop from cooking further.

❸ Place one serving of the noodles on a plate or in a bowl, pour a ladle of meat sauce in the middle, then arrange 25 g (1 oz) of each vegetable (per serving) all around the sauce.

包子家族

米饭和面条

担担面
DAN DAN NOODLES

MAKES AROUND 2 SERVINGS

INGREDIENTS

SICHUAN RED PEPPERS	10 G (¼ OZ)
DRIED CHILLI FLAKES	40 G (1½ OZ)
PEANUTS	20 G (¾ OZ)
PORK MINCE	120 G (4¼ OZ)
CHOPPED SPRING ONION	60 G (2¼ OZ)
SALT	10 G (¼ OZ)
+ A LITTLE FOR COOKING	
WHEAT NOODLES	250 G (9 OZ)
QUARTERED BOK CHOY	60 G (2¼ OZ)
SESAME PASTE	20 G (¾ OZ)
LIGHT SOY SAUCE	60 ML (¼ CUP)
VINEGAR	2 TABLESPOONS
WHITE (GRANULATED) SUGAR	10 G (¼ OZ)
SESAME OIL	1 TEASPOON
PRESERVED MUSTARD GREENS (YA CAI)	30 G (1 OZ)
OIL FOR FRYING	

GARNISH

CHOPPED SPRING ONION	3 STEMS
JULIENNED CARROT	
JULIENNED CUCUMBER	

❶ Fry the Sichuan red peppers in oil at 160°C (320°F) for 8 to 10 minutes until the seeds start to brown. ● Lower the heat to 150°C (300°F) and add the chilli flakes while stirring. ● Leave to cool.

❷ Lightly fry the peanuts in a frying pan over medium to high heat, then crush them.

❸ Pour a drizzle of oil into a frying pan over medium to high heat and fry the pork mince with the spring onion. ● Season with the extra salt and set aside.

❹ Cook the noodles according to the packet instructions, adding the bok choy 1 minute before the end of cooking. ● Drain, reserving a little of the cooking water, and transfer to a bowl. ● In another bowl, mix the sesame paste, 1 teaspoon of the reserved noodle cooking water, the soy sauce, vinegar, sugar, salt and sesame oil. ● Pour the sauce over the noodles, sprinkle with ya cai, crushed peanuts and add the pork. ● Strain the cooled chilli oil and drizzle over the noodles. ● Garnish with the spring onion, carrot and cucumber and serve.

包子家族

米饭和面条

麻酱面
COLD NOODLES WITH SESAME

MAKES AROUND 2 SERVINGS

INGREDIENTS

CARROT	100 G (3½ OZ)
CUCUMBER	100 G (3½ OZ)
BEAN SPROUTS	60 G (½ CUP)
FRESH NOODLES (WITHOUT EGGS)	300 G (10½ OZ)
CORIANDER	3 SPRIGS (STEMS AND LEAVES)
WHITE SESAME SEEDS	2 PINCHES

SAUCE

SESAME PASTE	55 G (2 OZ)
SESAME OIL	2 TEASPOONS
PEANUT BUTTER	20 G (¾ OZ)
LIGHT SOY SAUCE	4 TEASPOONS
BLACK VINEGAR	4 TEASPOONS
MIRIN	1 TABLESPOON
WHITE RICE VINEGAR	1 TABLESPOON

❶ Cut the carrot and cucumber into thin matchsticks, wash the bean sprouts and set aside.

❷ Cook the noodles according to the packet instructions and then refresh in iced water.

❸ Mix all the sauce ingredients together with a stick blender or whisk in a large bowl. ● If using a whisk, first mix the sesame paste and sesame oil with the peanut butter, before gradually adding the liquid ingredients.

❹ Add the noodles to the sauce and mix until well coated.

❺ Serve the noodles in a bowl topped with the fresh vegetables, coriander and sesame seeds.

包子家族

甜点

DESSERTS
243

甜点

黑芝麻包
BLACK SESAME BAO

MAKES AROUND 12 BAO

INGREDIENTS

BLACK SESAME SEEDS	255 G (9 OZ)
WHITE SESAME SEEDS	5 G (⅛ OZ)
BUTTER	125 G (½ CUP)
HONEY	150 G (5½ OZ)
BAO DOUGH (PAGE 86)	650 G (1 LB 7 OZ)
SALT	1 PINCH
OIL FOR FRYING (OPTIONAL)	

❶ Toast the sesame seeds in a dry frying pan or oven until the white sesame seeds are golden brown. ● Allow to cool, reserve 1 tablespoon for garnishing, then grind them in a blender (a finely ground blend will give the filling a better consistency and avoid getting as many sesame seeds stuck in your teeth after eating!).

❷ Melt the butter in a saucepan, then add the sesame seeds and honey. ● Stir until well combined and then set aside to cool in the refrigerator. ● When the mixture is solid but still soft enough to shape, form 35 g (1¼ oz) balls.

❸ Each bao should have 50 g (1¾ oz) dough and 35 g (1¼ oz) filling. ● Assemble according to the step-by-step instructions on pages 86–89. ● Let the bao stand in a warm, humid place for 20 minutes so that the dough can rise a second time. ● Steam for 12 minutes.

❹ Bao can be eaten once removed from the steamer. ● However, to get the signature Sesame Bao from the Bao Family, you can fry the bottom of the bao in oil until you get a beautiful golden colour (make sure the bottom is tightly closed to prevent any filling spilling into the hot oil). ● Serve sprinkled with extra sesame seeds and a pinch of salt on top.

包子家族

紅豆沙包
RED BEAN BAO

THIS RECIPE USES TRADITIONAL RED BEAN PASTE, WHICH IS MOSTLY VERY SWEET,
WITH LEMON AND SPICES ADDED. IT'S VERY SIMPLE, SUPER ADDICTIVE AND IT MAKES
A VERY GOOD BAO FOR DESSERT OR FOR A SNACK WHEN EATEN AT ROOM TEMPERATURE.

MAKES AROUND 12 BAO

INGREDIENTS

BUTTER .... 200 G (7 OZ)
WATER .... 40 ML (1¼ FL OZ)
RED BEAN PASTE .... 500 G (1 LB 2 OZ)
CONDENSED MILK .... 160 ML (5¼ FL OZ)

FRESHLY GROUND TIMUT PEPPER (OPTIONAL) .... 1 PINCH
GRATED LEMON ZEST .... 1 PIECE
BAO DOUGH (PAGE 86) .... 650 G (1 LB 7 OZ)

❶ Melt the butter in a saucepan, then pour in the water, red bean paste, condensed milk, ground timut pepper and grated lemon zest. ● Stir until well combined, heating over low heat if necessary, then leave to cool in the refrigerator. ● When the mixture is solid, but still soft enough to shape, form 40 g (1½ oz) balls.

❷ Each bao should have 50 g (1¾ oz) dough and 40 g (1½ oz) filling. ● Assemble according to the step-by-step instructions on pages 86–89. ● Let the bao stand in a warm, humid place for 20 minutes so that the dough can rise a second time.

❸ Steam for 12 minutes. ● Serve immediately.

OUR TIP

Bao can be eaten as soon as they come out of the steamer or at room temperature.

流沙包
'FLOWING SAND' BAO

MAKES AROUND 24 BAO

INGREDIENTS

SALTED DUCK EGG YOLKS	6
AGAR-AGAR	12 G (½ OZ)
CORNFLOUR	60 G (½ CUP)
WHITE (GRANULATED) SUGAR	200 G (7 OZ)
COCONUT MILK	500 ML (2 CUPS)
THICK (DOUBLE) CREAM	240 ML (8 FL OZ)
BUTTER	60 G (¼ CUP)
BAO DOUGH (PAGE 86)	1.3 KG (3 LB)

❶ Steam the egg yolks for 12 minutes, then crush using a fork. ● In a blender (or in a tall container, using a stick blender), blend the egg yolks, agar-agar, cornflour and 1 heaped tablespoon of sugar.

❷ In a deep saucepan, heat the coconut milk, cream and remaining sugar, without boiling.

❸ Transfer about a third of the hot liquid into the blender and blend until you get a smooth mixture. ● Return the mixture to the pan and, over medium to low heat, stir with a spatula to ensure the bottom doesn't stick. ● Once the mixture has thickened, transfer to a large bowl.

❹ Cut the butter into cubes, then stir into the mixture, piece by piece. ● If the butter remains separated, mix with a whisk. ● Allow to cool completely.

❺ Each bao should have 50 g (1¾ oz) dough and 40 g (1½ oz) filling. ● Assemble according to the step-by-step instructions on pages 86–89.

❻ Let the bao rest in a warm, humid place for 20 minutes to rise a second time (dough has already risen a first time after making).

❼ Steam for 10 minutes and serve.

包子家族

蛋挞
EGG TARTS

MAKES AROUND 15 TARTS

FILLING		DOUGH	
WHITE (GRANULATED) SUGAR	85 G (3 OZ)	SOFTENED BUTTER	150 G (5½ OZ)
HOT WATER	200 ML (7 FL OZ)	ICING SUGAR	50 G (1¾ OZ)
EGGS	2 (150 G/5½ OZ)	EGG	1
EVAPORATED MILK	120 ML (½ CUP)	MILK POWDER	10 G (¼ OZ)
VANILLA EXTRACT	1 TEASPOON	PLAIN FLOUR	250 G (1⅔ CUPS)
		SALT	2 G (¹⁄₁₆ OZ)

❶ Prepare the filling: dissolve the sugar in the hot water. ● Beat the eggs with the evaporated milk and vanilla extract, then add the mixture to the sugar liquid. ● Pass through a fine sieve to remove all air bubbles. ● Set aside.

❷ Prepare the dough: beat the butter with the icing sugar until a creamy, airy texture is obtained. ● Add the beaten egg and remaining dry ingredients. ● Mix with your hands until a dough forms, but be careful not to overwork it to prevent it from becoming too dense. ● Allow it to cool in the refrigerator until it has play-dough like consistency.

❸ Preheat the oven to 190°C (375°F). ● Using 8 cm (3¼ inch) tins or moulds or a muffin pan with 8 cm (3¼ inch) cups, shape 35 g (1¼ oz) dough per tart. ● Press the dough into the bottom of the cups or moulds with your thumb and pour the filling in to come halfway up the sides.

❹ Place in the oven for 6 minutes, then lower the temperature to 165°C (325°F) to finish cooking: the egg mixture must be cooked, and should be pale yellow in colour and lightly puffed.

汤圆
TANGYUAN

MAKES AROUND 18 TANGYUAN

FILLING

FAT (COCONUT OIL/PORK FAT/BUTTER)	**100 G (3½ OZ)**
CRUSHED BLACK SESAME SEEDS	**100 G (3½ OZ)**
WHITE (GRANULATED) SUGAR	**125 G (4½ OZ)**
PEANUT BUTTER	**100 G (3½ OZ)**
SESAME OIL	**1 TEASPOON**

DOUGH

GLUTINOUS (STICKY) RICE FLOUR	**160 G (5¾ OZ)**
RICE FLOUR	**20 G (¾ OZ)**
WATER	**140 ML (4¾ FL OZ)**
WHITE (GRANULATED) SUGAR	**20 G (¾ OZ)**
VEGETABLE OIL	**4 TEASPOONS**

GINGER SYRUP

SLICED GINGER	**20 G (¾ OZ)**
RAW SUGAR	**100 G (3½ OZ)**
WATER	**650 ML (22½ FL OZ)**

❶ Prepare the syrup: put all the ingredients in a saucepan and simmer for 10 minutes.

❷ Prepare the filling: bring the fat to room temperature to make it easier to work with. ● Mix the fat together with the remaining ingredients using a spoon. ● Form small 6 g (⅛ oz) balls and leave to rest in the refrigerator until firm.

❸ Prepare the dough: mix all the ingredients until a smooth dough is obtained. ● Divide it into 20 g (¾ oz) balls.

❹ To assemble, form a hollow in the centre of each dough ball with your thumb and insert a ball of filling. ● Wrap the dough around the filling, then roll using your hands to form a round ball.

❺ Cook the tangyuan in boiling water for 2 to 3 minutes. ● Once they rise to the surface, let them cook for another 1 to 2 minutes.

❻ Serve in the ginger syrup.

甜
点

西多士
HONG KONG FRENCH TOAST

MAKES 2 SERVINGS

INGREDIENTS

PEANUT BUTTER ....**4 TABLESPOONS**
SANDWICH BREAD ....**4 SLICES (CRUSTS REMOVED)**
OIL FOR FRYING .... **180 ML (¾ CUP)**
EGGS **3**

GARNISH

BUTTER ....**30 G (1 OZ)**
MAPLE SYRUP ....**4 TABLESPOONS**

❶ Spread the peanut butter on a slice of bread and cover with another slice of bread to form a sandwich. ● Repeat with the other two slices.

❷ In a deep pan, heat the oil to 180°C (350°F). ● Meanwhile, beat the eggs well, then pour them into a shallow bowl.

❸ Dip one sandwich at a time in the beaten egg, making sure all sides are covered. ● Gently place the sandwich in the hot oil and fry it for 2 minutes until you get a nice golden colour (the oil should be hot enough to lightly puff up the egg).

❹ Serve with a little butter and maple syrup.

包
子
家
族

炸鲜奶
FRIED MILK

MAKES 2 SERVINGS

INGREDIENTS

MILK .... 250 ML (1 CUP)
CORNFLOUR .... 60 G (½ CUP)
WHITE (GRANULATED) SUGAR .... 20 G (¾ OZ)
CONDENSED MILK .... 4 TEASPOONS

BAKING POWDER .... 10 G (¼ OZ)
WATER .... 100 ML (3½ FL OZ)
OIL FOR FRYING
PLAIN FLOUR FOR COATING

❶ Heat the milk, 30 g (¼ cup) cornflour, the sugar and condensed milk over low heat in a saucepan, stirring continuously until the mixture thickens. ● Transfer to a lightly oiled rectangular dish and leave to cool in the refrigerator for at least 1 hour.

❷ Heat the oil to 160°C (320°F). ● Meanwhile, cut 2 × 5 cm (¾ × 2 inch) rectangles from the milk mixture and coat the whole surface with flour. ● Prepare the coating by mixing the remaining cornflour, baking powder and water. ● Dip each milk rectangle in the coating, then carefully place them in the oil. ● Fry until the pieces are nice and golden. ● Remove any excess oil by placing each piece on paper towel. ● Enjoy warm.

甜点

绿豆馅麻团
SESAME BALLS WITH MUNG BEANS AND COCONUT

MAKES AROUND 12 PIECES

INGREDIENTS
SESAME SEEDS .... 150 G (5½ OZ)
OIL FOR FRYING

FILLING
SPLIT YELLOW MUNG BEANS .... 200 G (7 OZ)
WHITE (GRANULATED) SUGAR .... 120 G (4¼ OZ)
GRATED COCONUT .... 50 G (1¾ OZ)
BUTTER .... 40 G (1½ OZ)
SALT .... 1 PINCH

DOUGH
GLUTINOUS (STICKY) RICE FLOUR .... 400 G (14 OZ)
+ A LITTLE TO WORK THE DOUGH
RICE FLOUR .... 40 G (1½ OZ)
BAKING POWDER .... 12 G (½ OZ)
WHITE (GRANULATED) SUGAR .... 140 G (⅔ CUP)
SALT .... 1 PINCH
BOILING WATER .... 350 ML (12 FI OZ)

❶ Prepare the filling: soak the mung beans in a saucepan of cold water for 1 hour. ● Remove the water and pour in fresh water 1 to 2 cm (½ to ¾ inch) above the level of the beans. ● Bring to the boil over high heat, then lower the heat. ● Allow to simmer over low heat, stirring occasionally. ● When there is no more liquid and the mixture is boiling, remove from the heat. ● The beans should be cooked but not completely soft.

❷ Add the sugar and grated coconut. ● The mixture should have a purée-like consistency with bean chunks inside. ● Add the butter and salt, stir to combine, then place the mixture in the refrigerator.

❸ When the filling has firmed up and can be easily shaped, roll it into 25 g (1 oz) balls, pressing firmly to keep the filling together. ● Set aside in the refrigerator for 1 hour.

❹ Prepare the dough by mixing the glutinous rice flour, rice flour and baking powder in a bowl. ● Allow the sugar and salt to dissolve in the boiling water. ● Stir the water into the dry ingredients to combine. ● When all the water has been added, knead until the dough is smooth.

❺ To shape dough balls, it is useful to have a small bowl of water and a small amount of glutinous rice flour nearby, in case the dough is very dry or very wet. ● Take 35 g (1¼ oz) dough and roll it into a ball, then flatten between your palms. ● Place a ball of cooled filling in the centre, then wrap it completely with the dough. ● Try to keep an even thickness of dough around the ball to avoid having parts that are too thin and may burst during frying.

❻ When each ball is sealed, roll it in your hands to form a nice round shape, then coat them with sesame seeds.

❼ Fry the balls at 150°C (300°F) until they are nice and golden. ● Since these balls are quite dense, it is advisable to place a ball on a large slotted spoon, then lower it gently into the oil. ● A low temperature is recommended for frying so that the dough has time to cook before the outside becomes too crispy. ● Serve hot.

包子家族

拔丝苹果
APPLE FRITTERS WITH CARAMEL

MAKES AROUND 2 SERVINGS

INGREDIENTS

APPLES	2
EGG WHITE	60 G (2¼ OZ)
SALT	1 PINCH
CORNFLOUR	60 G (½ CUP)

VEGETABLE OIL	2 TEASPOONS
WHITE (GRANULATED) SUGAR	100 G (3½ OZ)
WATER	80 ML (⅓ CUP)
OIL FOR FRYING	

❶ Peel the apples and cut into quarters. ● Remove the core and cut each quarter in two lengthways to get 8 pieces (if your apples are big, cut them in 12). ● Then cut each quarter into 3 small pieces.

❷ In a bowl, mix the egg white, salt and cornflour until a smooth, runny mixture is obtained, then pour in the 2 teaspoons of oil.

❸ Place the apples into the mixture, then fry them in oil at 160°C (320°F). ● Once the fruit is golden, remove excess oil by draining them on paper towel.

❹ Dissolve the sugar in the water in a small saucepan or wok over medium heat. ● Allow to simmer gently until the syrup no longer contains water but before it caramelises (at this stage, the syrup should crystallise and break easily once cooled).

❺ Add all the fried apple pieces to the wok or pan, then stir to coat each piece with syrup.

❻ Serve immediately in a bowl, accompanied by a small bowl of iced water. ● Dip the fried caramelised pieces in iced water to set the caramel and enjoy.

包
子
家
族

茶文化
TEA CULTURE

Legend has it that an Emperor discovered tea during a walk in 2737 BC and, ever since, consuming tea has become embedded in Chinese civilisation and its traditions. Tea became an imperial drink from the eighth century onwards.

The tea tree was one of the first plants grown as a crop in China, in the region west of Yunnan. All types of tea (green, black, white) come from the *Camellia sinensis* plant, but it is the way the leaves are harvested that determines the type.

Drinking tea has become an art and a state of mind. It symbolises chan (*Zen*), self-control, hospitality, calm, refinement and elegance. Tea houses opened and became places of community and sharing, as well as part of cultural life through displays of art, opera or poetry. Drinking tea is a real experience in China; the quality of the tea is judged by its colour, aroma and flavour. The drinking experience is determined by the quality of the water and the teapot. The ceramics and porcelain used also impart the required aesthetic character to the experience.

HOW TO DRINK TEA?

● High-quality teas are consumed without sugar, milk or flavourings. ● All basic accessories (teapot and cups) must be scalded before preparing the tea. ● Tea leaves are rinsed in hot water quickly before the first infusion, to wash the leaves but also to allow the leaf to better develop its flavours. ● Slowly pour in hot water at the right temperature. ● For green and white tea: water at 80–85°C (176–185°F) for a 3 to 5 minute infusion, using 3 g for a small teapot. ● For Oolong tea: water at 90–100°C (194–212°F) for a short 1 minute infusion, using 6 g in a small clay teapot. ● For red tea: water at 90–95°C (194–203°F) for a 3 to 5 minute infusion, using 6 g in an 800 ml (28 fl oz) teapot. ● For Pu-erh tea: water at 100°C (212°F) for a 2 minute infusion, using 8 g in a small clay teapot. ● It is possible to keep making up to five or even six successive infusions following the first one. Successive infusions are drunk in very small cups and at a fairly steady pace, a few sips each time. ● Choose a small-sized porcelain or Yixing clay teapot as the porosity of these pots retains the tea flavours. Ideally one teapot is designated to be used for each type of tea.

索引

包子家族

鸣谢
ACKNOWLEDGEMENTS

This book is a crazy dream. The dream of sharing everything we love about Chinese cuisine and our traditions, through our eyes. This project is the result of six months' collaboration with passionate people, experts in their fields, who share our passion for cooking, travel and creating hubs of urban life. *Bao Family* is a project close to my heart and I want to thank all the people who put their hearts and souls into the creation of this book:

— *Bao Family* authors Carole Cheung, Lynda Zhu.
— Bao Family chefs Lucy Chen, Jessica Chan, Victor Zheng, Liming Shu, Leslie Chirino, Tenzin Choeknor, Rachel Jiang, Alyssa Fowler, Andrej Demeter, Hong Hai Tran, Alex (Dorjee Lodoe Rabutsang), Madame Chun.
— My partner Billy Pham, thank you for sharing this crazy adventure with me.

— All the Bao Family members who live out the Bao Vibe every day.
— Donald Choque and Yoann Le Goff, our wonderful designers from Atelier Choque Le Goff for the artistic direction.
— Agathe Hernandez, our superb stylist, who went to Chinatown in Paris and Marseille to source the crockery.
— Grégoire Kalt, who brought his photographer's eye to our cooking.
— Catherine Roig and Lisa Grall, who made this book possible.

And a special mention to the Bao Family members who make the Bao Vibe come to life every day: Yana, Christian, Vann, Thavinh, Hanna, Ema, Simon, Laura, Léa, Guido, Caesar, Adrien, Aurélie, and all their teams.

包
子
家
族

BAO RESTAURANTS

Petit Bao 116 rue Saint Denis, 75002 Paris
Gros Bao 72 Quai de Jemmapes, 75010 Paris
Bleu Bao 8 rue Saint Lazare, 75009 Paris
Bao Express & Bao Bakery 10 rue Bréguet, 75011 Paris

Published in 2023 by Murdoch Books, an imprint of Allen & Unwin
First published in 2022 by La Maison Hachette Pratique, an imprint of Hachette Livre, France

Murdoch Books Australia
Cammeraygal Country
83 Alexander Street
Crows Nest NSW 2065
Phone: +61 (0)2 8425 0100
murdochbooks.com.au
info@murdochbooks.com.au

Murdoch Books UK
Ormond House
26–27 Boswell Street
London WC1N 3JZ
Phone: +44 (0) 20 8785 5995
murdochbooks.co.uk
info@murdochbooks.co.uk

For corporate orders and custom publishing, contact our business development team at
salesenquiries@murdochbooks.com.au

Management: Catherine Saunier-Talec
Editorial Manager: Lisa Grall
Publisher representative: Catherine Roig
Project Manager: Jeanne Mauboussin
Art direction and illustrations: Workshop
  Choque Le Goff, assisted by Cédric Houssen
Photography: Grégoire Kalt
Styling: Agathe Hernandez
Text preparation: Charlotte Müller
Layout: The Paoists
Production Manager: Amélie Latsch

English-language edition:
Publisher: Céline Hughes
Translator: Nicola Thayil
Editor: Kay Halsey
Designer and cover
  designer: Sarah McCoy
Production Director: Lou Playfair

*Murdoch Books acknowledges the Traditional Owners of the Country on which we live and work.
We pay our respects to all Aboriginal and Torres Strait Islander Elders, past and present.*

ISBN 978 1 92261 667 8

A catalogue record for this
book is available from the
National Library of Australia

A catalogue record for this book is available from the British Library
Printed by C & C Offset Printing Co. Ltd., China

OVEN GUIDE: You may find cooking times vary depending on the oven you are using. The recipes
in this book are based on fan-assisted oven temperatures. For non-fan-assisted ovens, as a general rule,
set the oven temperature to 20°C (35°F) higher than indicated in the recipe.

TABLESPOON MEASURES: We have used 15 ml (3 teaspoon) tablespoon measures.

IMPORTANT: Those who might be at risk from the effects of salmonella poisoning (the elderly,
pregnant women, young children and those suffering from immune deficiency diseases) should
consult their doctor with any concerns about eating raw eggs. Please ensure that all seafood and
beef to be eaten raw or lightly cooked are very fresh and of the highest quality.

10 9 8 7 6 5 4 3 2 1

粤菜

GUANGDONG CUISINE

CHARACTERISTICS: LIGHT, UMAMI, DELICATE, FRESH, SWEET

There are many cooking methods in Guangdong, or Cantonese, cuisine, which are adapted to using fresh ingredients and retaining their attributes. Techniques include steaming, frying at high temperature, boiling, smothering and wok cooking. Spices or oil are used sparingly and dishes are not spicy so as to highlight the flavours of each ingredient. The most common seasonings used are coriander, ginger and pepper.

Cantonese cuisine is made up of Guangzhou cuisine, Chaoshan, or Teochew, cuisine and Hakka cuisine. Teochew cuisine is influenced by Fujian as well as Cantonese cuisine. It is present in Southeast Asia, as is Hakka cuisine due to migration. As they had to travel, the Hakka people attached more importance to the texture and taste of food than to appearance. They also consumed a lot of dried and pickled foods.

川菜

SICHUAN CUISINE

CHARACTERISTICS: RICH, HOT, SPICY, SWEET-AND-SOUR

Sichuan cuisine is the most popular cuisine in China. It is famous for being very spicy, although it should not be reduced to that.

As for cooking techniques, frying, steaming and smothering are preferred. Pickled or smoked vegetables are also popular. Sichuan cuisine contains a lot of chillies, ginger, garlic and Chinese five spice. Sichuan pepper, widely used in the region, imparts a tingly, numbing sensation to dishes – the hallmark of Sichuan cuisine. Spicy fermented bean paste (doubanjiang, 豆瓣酱) is also a staple food. It is the combination of all these ingredients that gives dishes a flavourful and powerful taste.

苏菜

JIANGSU CUISINE

CHARACTERISTICS: FRESH, DELICATE, LIGHT, UMAMI, SLIGHTLY SWEET

Jiangsu cuisine boasts over two millennia of history, yet it is probably the least known outside of China. The standard of living in the area is quite high, so the dishes often have a delicate appearance, and use quality products. Both saltwater and freshwater fish are common and seasonal products are preferred. Special attention is paid to preserving the natural flavours of the ingredients and to how they are cut. The most widely used cooking technique is stewing. Dishes have a combination of salty, umami and slightly sweet tastes.

Jiangsu cuisine is made up of several styles, often associated with a major city. Examples include Nanjing, Yangzhou, Suzhou, Huai'an, Xuzhou and Haizhou cuisines.

浙菜

ZHEJIANG CUISINE

CHARACTERISTICS: LIGHT, FRESH, DELICATE

The Zhejiang province is dominated by mountains and hills. It is one of the richest regions of China.

The cuisine of this region attaches great importance to the presentation of dishes. People enjoy using fresh produce, fish, seafood and seasonal vegetables. They consume a lot of raw or almost raw food, and the cooking techniques used are flash frying, wok cooking and steaming. Yellow wine is commonly used in seasonings and marinades.

Zhejiang cuisine can be divided into four major styles, each associated with one of the provincial cities: Shaoxing, whose wine is one of the best known varieties of yellow rice wine; Wenzhou; Ningbo, which focuses on the freshness and iodine taste of seafood, and is known for its pastry; and Hangzhou.